Targeted A   ed Effects

Ernest Cyril de Run

Targeted Advertising Unintended Effects

VDM Verlag Dr. Müller

Imprint

Bibliographic information by the German National Library: The German National Library lists this publication at the German National Bibliography; detailed bibliographic information is available on the Internet at http://dnb.d-nb.de.

Cover image: www.purestockx.com

Publisher:
VDM Verlag Dr. Müller Aktiengesellschaft & Co. KG, Dudweiler Landstr. 125 a, 66123 Saarbrücken, Germany,
Phone +49 681 9100-698, Fax +49 681 9100-988,
Email: info@vdm-verlag.de

Produced in USA and UK by:
Lightning Source Inc., La Vergne, Tennessee, USA
Lightning Source UK Ltd., Milton Keynes, UK
BookSurge LLC, 5341 Dorchester Road, Suite 16, North Charleston, SC 29418, USA

ISBN: 978-3-639-06100-0

ABSTRACT

Although, advertising has been a major area of study in marketing, limited research investigating the unintended effects of targeted advertising beyond social and moral issues has been conducted. This research contributes to the current body of knowledge by examining the unintended effects of ethnically targeted advertising on ethnic groups that are not targeted, but who are still likely to see the advertising. The research also develops a holistic model for measuring the effects of targeted advertising using four variables; emotions, attitude to the advertisement, attitude to the company and behavioural intentions. The conceptual basis of the model is accommodation theory, which allows for different levels of targeting based on the language mix used in advertisements (e.g. ranging from advertisements that are solely in the targeted group language to advertisements with a mixture of languages to advertisements that are solely in the non-targeted group's language). The model was tested on three different ethnic groups in Malaysia.

Five key propositions were tested during the research: 1. That targeted advertisements will elicit negative unintended reactions from ethnic groups that are not targeted (P_1); 2. That there will be a direct relationship between the strength of reactions and the degree of language accommodation (i.e. those not targeted will have stronger negative reactions to advertisements that accommodate the targeted ethnic group) (P_2); 3. That "novel" advertisements with unexpected combinations of language and cultural cues, will elicit more negative reactions from those not targeted rather than "standard" advertisements with more commonly used combinations of language and cultural cues (P_3); 4. That there will be significant differences within ethnic groups in their reactions to targeted advertisements (P_4); 5. That there will be significant differences between ethnic groups in their reactions to targeted advertisements (P_5).

A factorial design was used to analyse the data collected by a survey. The factorial design consisted of five different advertisement types (by language), three different ethnicities, ethnic identification strength and measures of social distance. The dependent variables used were attitude towards the company, corporate credibility, corporate image, rapport, attitude towards the advertisement, affective response towards the advertisement, attitude towards the product, attitude towards the brand, purchase intention, word of mouth, overall emotions, alienation, anger, feeling targeted and perceived threat.

Test for P_1 supported the proposition of negative responses by non-targeted ethnic groups, albeit a lot of these were affective response. The findings also suggested that ethnic dominance and the social and cultural context might have mediated the level of negative response. Test for P_2 showed that the strength of negative reactions was not necessarily directly linked to the level of language accommodation. Test for P_3 showed that "novel" advertisements created stronger negative reactions among non-targeted ethnic groups than 'standard' advertisements. Test for P_4 showed that within group effects were minimal. The interactions posited for P_5 did not occur.

The theoretical implications of this research include support for a "holistic" approach to targeted advertising. In other words, instead of the previous view that looked at targeting as the end product, the research suggests that there are more factors to consider after targeting is implemented. The research also develops a model for assessing the unintended reactions of those not targeted. The findings indicate that there are limits to Accommodation Theory, Distinctiveness Theory and the concept of cultural schema. This research also has managerial implications and identifies actions that can be taken to reduce the negative reactions of non-targeted ethnic groups to ethnically targeted advertising and towards the company itself.

ACKNOWLEDGEMENTS

First and foremost I give thanks to God for his blessings, grace and mercy to me throughout all the days of my life. My thanks and gratitude to my wife, Doren Gibson Mengkoh, for her support, understanding and perseverance; my son, Walter Sangking de Run, for his smile; and my daughter Sarah Alvina de Run for being her.

I am grateful to my all that have helped in one-way or another in the creation of this book. Special thanks goes to Professor Brendan Gray, Mr. Brian Niven, Associate Professor Dr Kim Shyan Fam, Associate Professor Dr Scott Koslow, Associate Professor Sheelagh Matear, Mr Damien Mather, Mr. Neil Paul Sakai, Associate Professor Shazali Abu Mansor, Natthawut Srikantayoo, Michael Ottenbacher, Vincent Hassan, Marco Grix, Andrew Mitchell, Thorsk Westphal, Reverend Tim Hurd, Jo Dodd, May White, Siti Hasnah Hassan, Khadijah Mohd Tuah, Jennie Coleman, the late Kenneth Gray, Merle Gray, and Vaughan Gray.

Special thanks goes to family; my mum, Maurine Alvina O'Keeffe, brother Peter Claude de Run and his family, sister Shirley Anna de Run and her family, uncle Claude O'Keeffe, and father in-law Mr. Gibson Mengkoh and family.

Thank you.

3

TABLE OF CONTENTS

LIST OF TABLES

LIST OF FIGURES

LIST OF APPENDICES

1. INTRODUCTION

Effective Marketing: Segmenting and Targeting

Practitioners and academics have long believed that segmenting markets and targeting specific customer groups is the basis of effective marketing. The potential to classify and organize consumers into small, manageable, homogenous groups, i.e. segmenting, is attractive. Segmenting allows for targeting thus allowing a business's products, services, promotions and activities, to be directed to a specific group for the best possible outcome (Kotler & Armstrong, 1994). Theory posits that if products can be differentiated to cater for the needs of specific groups, their perceived superior quality will command higher prices and generate more repeat purchases with less advertising, thus lowering costs and boosting profits (Kotler & Armstrong, 1994; Samiee & Roth, 1992; Von der Fehr & Stevik, 1998).

Nevertheless, while segmenting and targeting appears to be important, much of the research in these areas has been superficial, normative and repetitive (Cooper & Lane, 1997; Hooley, Saunders, & Piercy, 1998; Pinson & Jinnett, 1993). Some writers state that brand differentiation is unlikely and that advertisements cannot persuade and merely reinforce attitudes and behaviors (Barnard & Ehrenberg, 1997; Ehrenberg, 2001; Ehrenberg, Barnard, & Scriven, 1997) minimizing the possibility of effective targeting. Targeting also presupposes that a particular group is important (Barnard & Ehrenberg, 1997). Segmentation, which forms the basis of targeting, has been criticized as not being workable, thus rendering targeting unattainable and supporting the view that it would be better to aim to please the masses (Kennedy & Ehrenberg, 2001).

Other authors have drawn attention to the fact that advertising is a form of mass communication that allows for the possibility that anyone may see it (Barnard & Ehrenberg, 1997; R. W. Pollay, 1986). Advertising utilizes mass media and therefore cannot be limited in order to be only seen by those whom a business wants it to be seen by, even if it is placed in specific targeted media (Cornwell, 1994; Ringold, 1995). Translation and other effects, such as language, ethnicity and acculturation, may create further problems for companies involved in cross-cultural marketing. Of prime concern must be unintended negative responses by non-target ethnic groups that may view ethnically targeted advertising.

Unintended Effects

Two types of unintended effects have been identified. The first type consist of any negative reactions by and consequences for those whom the advertisement specifically targets (Crain, 2002; M. E. Goldberg & Gorn, 1978; Preston, 1999; Prothrow-Stith & Spivak, 1998). The second type consist of negative reactions by and consequences for those not targeted but who may have seen advertisements that target other groups (Preston, 1999; Rotfled, 1999). Reactions to advertisements by teenagers (Martin & Gentry, 1997), girls and young women (Martin & Gentry, 1997; Martin & Kennedy, 1993) have been the focus of many previous studies.

10

The discussion of unintended effects of advertising in literature almost exclusively focuses on social and moral issues. These include issues such as a sense of inadequacy on women's self-concepts, while reinforcing a preoccupation with physical attractiveness (Gulas & McKeage, 2000; Myers & Biocca, 1992), reinforcing physical attractiveness, self esteem, financial success and materialism (M. E. Goldberg & Gorn, 1978; Martin & Kennedy, 1993; Richins, 1996), eating disorders (Gilly, 1999; R. T. Peterson, 1987), status seeking, social stereotypes, short sightedness, selfishness, a preoccupation with sexuality, conformity and a narrow view of reality that affects values, taste and culture (Ottesen, 1981; R. W. Pollay, 1986; Richins, 1991, 1996).

The issue of targeted versus non-targeted (adapted or standardized) advertisements has been discussed in the international advertising literature for a long time (Agrawal, 1995). Researchers have judged adaptation or standardization based on the performance of companies that follow either ideology (Albaum & Tse, 2001; Samiee & Roth, 1992; Szymanski, Bharadwaj, & Varadarajan, 1993). Only a few studies have investigated this issue from the perspective of the consumer (Shoham, 1996; Somasundaram & Light, 1994). Even fewer studies, have noted the reactions of those who see advertisements that have been adapted for other targeted groups. International marketing studies have only noted the reactions of targeted audiences and these reactions have tended to be limited to attitudes towards the advertisement and have neglected attitudes towards the firm.

Why this Book

This book examines the impact on a company, with advertisements adapted for a particular ethnic group, when viewed by those not targeted. A conceptual model (refer to Figure 1) was developed to diagnose affective and behavioral effects, based on relevant theories in the communications and advertising literatures. This is important because academics have tended to limit the study of unintended effects of targeted advertising to ethical, moral and social issues. Companies undertake targeting without realizing the full force of their actions or the potential reactions of those currently not targeted, but who may, in the future become customers. Given this situation, this book proposes an alternative "holistic" method to evaluating the outcome of targeted advertising for a company.

This book is an investigation into a popular advertising practice (ethnically targeted advertising) that could cause unintended harm to a firm in the long-term. The potential negative reactions of viewers of ethnically targeted advertising that will be assessed in this book (affect, attitude to the advertisement, attitude to the company and behavioral intention) have all been used in previous studies of advertising effectiveness and/or firm performance. The key underlying assumption of this book is that negative responses of viewers to these measures (i.e. the dependent variables in the model) could cause long-term (if not short-term) harm to the company responsible for the targeted advertising being studied.

Five propositions were developed to provide a thorough examination of the unintended effect of ethnically targeted advertising on those not targeted. The specific objectives identified are as follows:

1. Targeting
To determine whether the unintended effects of ethnically targeted advertising are significant enough to warrant companies taking precautionary measures when using targeted advertising;

2. Accommodation
To investigate the impact of various levels of accommodation to an ethnically targeted group and the reactions of those ethnic groups not accommodated by these advertisements;

3. Dominant and Non-Dominant Ethnic Groups' Reactions To "Novel" and "Standard" Advertisements
To compare the reactions of non-targeted groups to "novel" (advertisements with unexpected combination of language and cultural cues) and "standard" (advertisements with more commonly used combinations of language and cultural cues) advertisements based on ethnic dominance;

4. Within Group Differences
To scrutinize the difference in reaction within ethnic groups when they see ethnically targeted advertisements, using ethnic identification strength to measure within group effects;

5. Between Group Differences
To examine the impact of targeting on the reaction between ethnic groups using social distance to measure between group effects.

Context for the Book

Advertisements can target any group of people, who may be segmented by ethnicity, demographics, socio-economic variables, psychographics, or a combination of various factors (Solomon, 1999). This research is conducted in the context of advertisements that fully target a particular ethnic group (the Iban), and partially target two other ethnic groups (the Malay and the Chinese) in Malaysia.

Malaysia is a multi-ethnic country in South East Asia. It has a population of 23.27 million, where the majority of the population is Malay (50%), followed by Chinese (26%), Indians (7.7%) and Iban (1.8%). However in Sarawak itself, the Iban are the majority (30.1%) followed by Chinese (26.7%) and Malay (23%) (Anonymous, 2004).

Malays are defined as people who speak Malay, lead the Malay way of life and are of the Islamic faith (O. Asmah, 1983) and endogamy seems to be the rule (O. Asmah, 1983; Purcell, 1965). They are believed to have migrated from Yunnan (O. Asmah, 1983) or Sumatra (H. O. Asmah, 1977). Malays are the largest ethnic group in Malaysia (Andaya & Andaya, 1982; O. Asmah, 1983; Mardiana, 2000). Malay social interaction is limited to the extended family unit with contacts with other ethnic groups such as Chinese and Indian limited for the purposes of trade (Nazaruddin, Ma'rof, Asnarulkhadi, & Ismail, 2001; Purcell, 1965). The Malay language belongs to the Austronesian stock with a number of regional dialects (H. O. Asmah, 1977; O. Asmah, 1983).

The Chinese in Malaysia are mainly descendants of immigrants from the southern coastal provinces of China (K. H. Lee & Tan, 2000; Nazaruddin et al., 2001). The Chinese tend to be urban, but are nearly everywhere, in town and village alike (Purcell, 1965). In 1957, there were 2,332,963 Chinese (37.1%) in Malaysia (Nazaruddin et al., 2001) and while the number has increased, the percentage is now at around 26%. Mandarin is the written and spoken language learnt at school but there are numerous spoken dialect groups (K. H. Lee & Tan, 2000). The Chinese have been economically dominant in the commercial sector (Andaya & Andaya, 1982; Chew, 1941; Mardiana, 2000), with daily contact with other races for trade purposes (Purcell, 1965). They are followers of various religions and practice endogamy (O. Asmah, 1983; Hodder, 1959; Purcell, 1965).

The Iban are a riverine group of rice cultivators inhabiting the interior hill country of Sarawak and parts of Indonesian Borneo (J. D. Freeman, 1955). The name "Iban" is from the Kayan language and means "immigrant" (J. D. Freeman, 1958). The most common Iban settlement is the longhouse, comprising 4 to 50 independent family units. They are classless but very status-conscious. The Iban religion revolves around augury, omens and rice with a small number converted to Christianity (Low, 1848; Pringle, 1970; H. L. Roth, 1896). The Iban have long been in contact with other groups and are well known for their social encouragement of initiative and free collective participation (D. Freeman, 1981). The Iban speak a dialect of Malay (Malayan subfamily, Austronesian family) that is distinct from other Bornean languages (Noriah, 1994).

Ethnicity was chosen as the segmentation basis for this research because there exists a wealth of ethnicity literature, ranging from sociological (Armstrong, 1999; Brumbaugh, 1995; White & Burke, 1987), to psychological studies (Alba & Moore, 1982; Brand, Ruiz, & Padilla, 1974; Caltabiano, 1984; Phinney, 1990). This allows for an understanding as to how ethnic groups react and therefore assist in the design of a controllable and explainable experiment.

Ethnic marketing is enthusiastically promoted to cross-cultural marketers as the best method to obtain customers (Dunn, 1992; Mummert, 1995; Steere, 1995). Ethnicity is described as a dynamic and popular method of targeting (Armstrong, 1999; Cui, 1997; Fost, 1990; Kinra, 1997; Kumar, 2002; Livingston, 1992). However, this 'gung-ho' approach needs to be moderated by a better understanding of the overall effects on companies that target specific ethnic groups.

Nevertheless, companies have recognized the need to target specific ethnic groups as they are potential markets, especially in the USA, where the Asian and Hispanic market is only now being noticed (Anonymous, 1999; Buck, 1998; Cantwell, 2001; Fost, 1990). Ethnicity is seen as a driver for several marketing trends in the United States, with the proliferation of ethnic media helping companies to reach these groups more effectively (Delener & Neelankavil, 1990; Gazdik, 1998; Lipski, 1985; O'Guinn, Faber, & Meyer, 1985; Roslow & Nicholls, 1996).

An ethnic segmentation was chosen for this research because it could mimic a real advertising campaign in Malaysia. In Malaysia, there are advertisements in all the three languages used in this experiment, (Iban, Malay and Chinese), as well as the necessary ethnic media that could carry such advertisements. Therefore it would not be something that is uncommon and unusual for respondents to react to.

Since the research is set in Malaysia, ethnicity is seen as crucial in examining and understanding the functioning and viability of its multi-cultural society (Abraham, 1999). Ethnic divisions are obviously visible in Malaysia and are based on language use (J. Platt, 1981; Watson, 1980b), in both formal and informal situations (Abraham, 1999). The ethnic diversity in Malaysia is divisive with individual ethnicities having their own perception of social reality (Milne, 1978). This can be utilized in a targeted promotional campaign.

Figure 1 Preliminary Conceptual Model to Diagnose Consumers' Reactions to Targeted Advertising

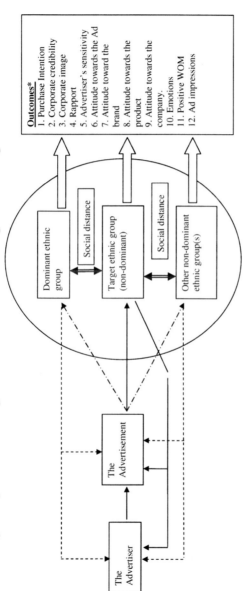

* Note: The reactions of the targeted group to the advertisements and to the company are likely to be positive, but the reactions of the non-targeted (dominant and non-dominant) ethnic groups are likely to be negative.

15

Issues Looked Into

Intended and Unintended Effects of Mass Communication
Questions have been raised about the strength, degree, incidence and type of effects of mass media communications (D. McQuail, 1983). Communication effect is said to have occurred if "as a consequence of a communication process, there is/is not in the individual mind something that would be/would not be there without it" (Piatila, 1977):125). An effect is basically a change that can be either planned or unplanned. Change is relative and related to time (long term or short term effects) as well as to the level of change (major or minor effects). It should be noted, however, that some mass media communications are geared to maintain the status quo (D. McQuail, 1983; Windahl, Signitzer, & Olson, 1992).

The intended effects of mass communication include surveillance, integration and correlation, entertainment and play, cultural continuity and mobilization (Berger, 1995). A number of studies have discussed other intended effects such as change (Piatila, 1977), reinforcement of beliefs (Lazarfeld, Berelson, & Gaudet, 1944), enlargement effects (De Fleur & Ball-Rokeach, 1982), cognitive complexity effects (Pavlik, 1987), reciprocal effects (Lang & Lang, 1986), the boomerang effect (Devito, 1986), spill-over effects (Lang & Lang, 1986), third-person effects (Davison, 1983), agenda setting effects (McCombs & Shaw, 1972) and cultivation effects (Gerbner, Gross, Morgan, & Signorielli, 1980). These effects are seen to influence three areas of society: the first is the available stock of knowledge, values, opinions and culture; the second relates to media selection and response; the third includes socialization, reality definition, distribution of knowledge and social control (D. McQuail, 1983).

Advertisements are a form of message transference using mass media and as such, suffer the same pitfalls and success as mass communications. An advertisement is designed professionally with a specific purpose of reinforcing certain behaviors and values (R. W. Pollay & Gallagher, 1990) and may not desire change but may aim to maintain the status quo (D. McQuail, 1983; Windahl et al., 1992). The intended effects of an advertisement are usually direct such as influencing sales of products or services, or indirect, such as improving product or service brand image (Ottesen, 1981). Other objectives of advertisements include providing product and brand information; inducing consumers to take action; reminding; and reinforcing previous messages (Wells, Burnett, & Moriarty, 2002).

Nevertheless, whatever meaning an advertiser wishes to convey to a targeted group, advertising will almost certainly be seen by others who are not targeted (R. W. Pollay, 1986). As posited earlier, there may be unintended negative responses from non-targeted groups.

Standardize or Adapt?
Targeting is also discussed in the international advertising literature. The central question is whether companies should standardize (not specifically target), or adapt (target), their advertisements (Agrawal, 1995). Another strongly debated issue is the performance of firms that use either standardized or adapted advertisements or market strategies (Jain, 1989; Keegan, Still, & Hill, 1987; M. S. Roth, 1995; Samiee & Roth, 1992; Shoham, 1996; Szymanski et al., 1993). However, the literature does not

identify the unintended effects of either standardized or adapted advertisements on those not targeted.

Communication Models and the Speech Accommodation Theory (SAT)

In order to understand how an advertisement may contribute to unintended effects, it is necessary to understand how communication occurs. Early communication models only portrayed the message sender, message and message receiver. Circular models, that took feedback into consideration then followed. One of the well-known communication models that deal with feedback is the Osgood-Schramm circular model (Berger, 1995). Generally these models depict a message as being constructed by the sender according to his/her expectations of the receiver. The sender will utilize his/her body of knowledge, vocabulary and common experience to craft the message (Burke, 1969; Corbett, 1965). Receivers of the message will use the same body of cultural knowledge to read the message, infer the sender's intentions and evaluate the message (McQuarrie & Mick, 1992; D. Mick & Buhl, 1992; Scott, 1990).

The Speech Accommodation Theory (SAT), on the other hand, highlights the importance of the sender and how the recipient views the sender (H. Giles, Taylor, & Bourhis, 1973). The SAT has two parts: the first involves the speaker who makes his/her style similar to that of the audience, in order to integrate the audience and the speaker and to obtain a favorable response (H. Giles et al., 1973) whereas the second part involves the audience response. It is too naïve to state that there is a direct relationship between an accommodating speaker and his/her audience response. However, this theory relates well to this research as it is concerned with the actions of the message sender (the company), in trying to accommodate (target) the receiver (consumer), as well as how the message receiver views (reacts to) the actions of the sender. This research will investigate the relationship between the level of accommodation and expected response in the context of advertisements aimed at a particular ethnic group. The SAT will be useful to assess the level of targeting to determine if there is any relationship between the level of accommodation and the response of non-target groups who are exposed to the target group advertisements.

Why is it Important to Understand the Issue in Question?

Some marketing practitioners and academics may question the importance of considering those that they are not currently targeting. However, those who adopt a broader 'stakeholder' view of the firm (Argandona, 1998; Wallace, 2003), or who are concerned about corporate social responsibility (Murphy & Crowther, 2002; Vos, 2003), or corporate reputation (Brouillard, 1983; P. Herbig & Milewicz, 1996), may argue otherwise.

There are also pragmatic reasons as to why we should be concerned with this issue.

Writers in recent years have begun to note the reactions of unintended (i.e. non-target group) audiences to advertising. Studies have included the reaction of gays to advertising targeting them, the viewpoint of companies advertising to the gay community, their fear of a backlash from the non-gay community (S. M. Kates, 1997, 1999, 2000; S. M. Kates & Belk, 2001) and the responses of heterosexual consumers to homosexual imagery in advertising (Bhat, Leigh, & Wardlow, 1998). Other researchers have looked at how non-targeted groups react emotionally to billboards targeting other groups (Touchstone, Homer, & Koslow, 1999), how they interpret such advertising and their attitudes towards the advertisements (Aaker, Brumbaugh, & Grier, 2000; S. A. Grier & Brumbaugh, 1999). Research has also been carried to examine how those not targeted react to different promotional pricing strategies (Feinberg, Krishna, & Zhang, 2002). Although the literature is beginning to note the responses from non-targeted groups, it has ignored the impact of unintended advertising effects on the companies involved. Most studies continue to focus on the reactions of the targeted groups.

It is clear that non-targeted groups have opportunities to see targeted promotions (Barnard & Ehrenberg, 1997; R. W. Pollay, 1986). They also form their own personalized views of such promotional activities (D. Mick & Buhl, 1992; D. Mick & Politi, 1989). Groups of people differ in their affinities, abilities, purposes and prejudices and as a result, each group will look at an advertisement differently and develop its own shared reactions and interpretation (S. A. Grier & Brumbaugh, 1999; Scott, 1994a). The varied meanings derived from the same message results from individuals' efforts to create order in their own lives (Csikszentmihalyi & Beattie, 1979; G. A. Kelly, 1955; B. M. Smith, Bruner, & White, 1956). As targeted advertising will still reach many audiences, any effects on company image and performance will depend on who is 'reached' and their derived meaning of the advertisement.

A question often raised by researchers concerned with segmentation and targeting is whether targeting gives a higher return compared to other approaches such as mass marketing or the shotgun approach (Cahill, 1997; M. Wright, 1996). One case study showed targeted promotions could be effective, but also noted that the business was clearly less strong in areas where advertising was not focused (K. M. Freeman, 1992). Claims for a superior return as a result of targeting appear debatable, as there is no method to determine the gain or loss from those not targeted (Cahill, 1997). A holistic approach to targeted advertising and a model to gauge the reaction of those targeted and not targeted may provide a clearer picture.

It has been shown that targeted advertisements can create negative emotions from those not targeted (Touchstone et al., 1999). Any emotional response generated in the viewing of an advertisement can affect a viewer's attitude towards the advertisement, attitude towards the brand and even purchase decisions (Batra & Ray, 1986; Holbrook & Batra, 1987). As such, by utilizing targeted advertising, a company may inadvertently generate negative attitudes towards the advertisement and brand, and reduce the purchase decisions of those not targeted. This is particularly important for firms with multiple segments and/or firms, which intend to expand into new segments in the future.

This issue may seem insignificant if a company has only one product and is targeting only one consumer group. In reality, this is rare. Most firms have multiple products and target multiple segments. If people not targeted by a company's advertisement also purchase other products, or even the same product, from that company, then the company image, customer rapport and performance may suffer if unintended audiences react negatively to an advertisement that targets another group. Even if a consumer currently does not purchase the company's product, the negative connotations implied by the advertisement will impede the consumer's views and purchase intentions in the future. The company will also have problems marketing the brand nationally and distributing it through national retail chains, as this will run counter to its current targeted promotional strategy with its limited coverage (K. M. Freeman, 1992).

In theory, a company may have its own loyal customers who are few in number but large in sales (i.e. the 80/20 rule) and more cost effective to reach (Underhill, 1994). However, there is continuous leakage of customers and erosion of any brand's repeat purchasing over a long period of time and companies must continuously recruit new customers (Anschuetz, 2002; Barnard & Ehrenberg, 1997). Instead of totally loyal customers, a company's customers are likely to be the company's competitors' customers too (Barnard and Ehrenberg, 1997). Therefore if the advertisement is not to their liking, they may easily purchase other brands within their defined set of acceptable brands.

A company's customers are the main advertising audience. Nonetheless, advertising audiences can be divided into four types: loyal customers, switchers, non-users and emergent customers (Steward, 1994). Non-users of a product are usually not worth reaching. Loyal customers are easy to reach and essential to keep. Switchers are fickle, but advertising to them can quickly boost sales. However, advertisements that target switchers may upset those that are loyal (Mohl, 2002). The most important group may be emergent consumers who are forming lifelong preferences. However, current advertising, targeting other audiences, may negatively influence emergent customers.

2. ADVERTISING

What is Advertising?

Advertising has been defined as a paid, mass-mediated attempt to persuade (O'Guinn, Allen, & Semenik, 2003). It is the art of presenting a product in the most favorable and convincing manner so as to create among the target audience (consumers) an intense desire to acquire the product (Morais, 1996). An advertisement is designed to reinforce certain behaviors and values (R. W. Pollay & Gallagher, 1990) with a specific intended effect (Ottesen, 1981; Wells et al., 2002). It may also desire no change but aim instead to maintain the status quo (D. McQuail, 1983; Windahl et al., 1992).

This book looks specifically at print advertising, which has its own peculiarities that must be noted. In print advertising there exists a separation by both time and space/place between the reader and the communicator (Bell, 1991; Suchan & Dulek, 1988). Once a print message is sent, it cannot be modified immediately. Feedback is nearly non-existent, difficult and slow to obtain. This distinction differentiates the "audience" from the "reader." An "audience" is involved in a dynamic environment in which the speaker obtains immediate feedback and adjusts his/her message accordingly. A "reader" is separated by both time and space/place from the communicator and would therefore find it difficult to communicate immediately with the message sender (Suchan & Dulek, 1988).

An important feature of print advertisements is the use of visual imagery effects as compared to the use of words alone which is a rarity. Visual images lead to more elaboration by readers and to more favorable attitudes toward the advertisement, without being difficult to comprehend (McQuarrie & Mick, 1999). However the picture must be congruent with the wordings (D. Luna & Peracchio, 2001), copy (Schmitt, Tavassoli, & Millard, 1993) and culture (McQuarrie & Mick, 1999) for it to have an impact.

It is rare for a print advertisement to not have a picture, as pictures have been shown to improve memory (Schmitt et al., 1993; Shepard, 1967; Starch, 1966). This is consistent with (Paivio, 1971) the dual-coding memory theory, which states that recall is enhanced if information is encoded in two systems (verbal and imagery) rather than one (usually verbal). Pictures are used to illustrate the brand and product in order to obtain better recall (McKelvie & MacGregor, 1996). However in the case of bilingual consumers, the visual image must be consistent with the wordings to help in the comprehension of the second language (D. Luna & Peracchio, 2001).

Images in advertisements are cognitively processed and are not absorbed peripherally or automatically (Scott, 1994b). The issue of relevant cultural knowledge on both sides (sender and receiver) is imperative for normative interaction and persuasion and to allow for cognitive processing (McQuarrie & Mick, 1992, 1999; D. Mick & Buhl, 1992; Scott, 1990, 1994b; Stern, 1990). The way a message is conveyed (pictorially or verbally), whether there are reference points for encoding the picture and the type of claim made affect the processing of an advertisement, which then affects the viewer's brand attitudes and purchase intentions (Edell & Staelin, 1983).

Given these factors, it is clear that by utilizing print advertisements, there are various factors such as visual images, language and culture that act as caveats that affect the viewers' reactions to advertisements and to the company. The issues of language, culture and cultural knowledge stand out. A reader must be able to encode advertisements to his or her own understanding before being able to react. A major problem for an advertiser, particularly those who target, is that the intended meaning may not be conveyed.

The Meaning of an Advertisement

Humans possess the only tool that makes social construction of reality possible, language. The reality and meaning of an advertisement is conveyed by the visual imagery, language used and the culture portrayed. All communication exists within a cultural context and communication is meaningful because of the culture framing it (Hecht, Collier, & Ribeau, 1993). There are two views as to how this occurs; the mapping view and the reality-construction view (Grace, 1987). The mapping view sees a common world, with language as analogous to maps of the world, fixed and determined. The reality-construction view, on the other hand, acknowledges the imperfection of our access to knowledge of the real world and posits that with our limited senses, we try to make sense of the real world using models that are reflected in our speech.

The reality-construction view came into prominence through the work of Benjamin Lee Whorf. Whorf identified that there are links between language, thought and culture (Whorf, 1941). This has been extended into the Sapir-Whorf hyporesearch of linguistic relativity, where language is seen as playing a role in making the world understood and interpreted. The Sapir view states that that all languages are equal, as there is no significant difference in language structure (Holmes, 1992). The schemas, by which the world is known and understood, are also the schemas by which advertisements are understood. These schemas are based on the Sapir-Whorf hyporesearch (Whorf, 1956) which postulates that language influences thought and the perception of reality. The Sapir-Whorf hyporesearch gives language a dominant role in shaping our views of the world. This hyporesearch suggests that each culture's language acts as a prism that we use to make sense of the world (Berger, 1995).

Sapir-Whorf's views on language have been challenged as not portraying social reality (Clark & Clark, 1977; Foss & Hakes, 1978). Nevertheless differences exist between languages of different ethnic groups (J. B. Carroll, 1963; J. B. Carroll & Casagrande, 1958; Fountain, 1999; Wassmann & Dasen, 1998). Others argue that language cannot be separated from its social-cultural context as it has significant bearing on the meanings communicated (Servaes, 1989). Other researchers have found psychological foundations for accepting the relaxed version of Sapir-Whorf's hyporesearch that language influences thought (Hunt & Agnoli, 1991).

The reality-construction view can be seen from the example of a bilingual reader's perspective. Articulate bilinguals have determined that they think differently in different languages. (Wierzbicka, 1985a) said that she is a different person in Polish and English and believes that the language she uses affects her attitudes and interpersonal behavior. She also demonstrates that linguistic differences are associated with culture differences and are extremely ethnocentric ((Wierzbicka, 1985b).

When looking at print advertisements, readers have to construct the reality and meaning of the advertisement without the aid of a speaker or message sender. Readers develop an assortment of meanings through the construction and deconstruction of advertising images. While readers know that advertisements present the world in an idealized way, they still draw meaning from the images (E. C. Hirschman & Thompson, 1997). However, some researchers believe that the meanings drawn from advertisements are distorted (R. W. Pollay, 1986; R. W. Pollay & Gallagher, 1990).

Studies have also shown that print advertisements affect how consumers perceive the advertiser as well as the advertisement (Koslow, Shamdasani, & Touchstone, 1994). Also, the use of a different language in another culture may create negative attitudes and low comprehension among the ethnic groups (Gerritsen, Korzilius, Van Meurs, & Gijsbers, 2000). This is partly due to structural differences in the languages used (Schmitt, Pan, & Tavassoli, 1994) and the different worldviews and social connotations each reader has (Appleman & Muysken, 1987; Whorf, 1956). Different worldviews and social connotations are reflected in such things as face saving (Ho, 1972) and time perspectives (Hall, 1976).

These differences in meaning creation provide an opportunity for unintended effects to occur. These unintended effects have mainly been shown as affecting social, moral and even physical outcomes (Downs & Harrison, 1985; Martin & Gentry, 1997; R. W. Pollay, 1986; R. W. Pollay & Gallagher, 1990). The literature recognizes that these effects exist, but researchers have yet to develop a method of detailing the outcomes from a marketing perspective.

Targeted Promotions

It is apparent that advertisements have meaning and that the reader derives meaning through various cultural and social means. It must also be understood that in the context of mass media communication, readers are not "masses" of individuals. Instead, readers are made up of various groupings that come together, to consume mediated texts, for a variety of reasons. Instead of masses, the term "publics" has been offered and defined as groups of people who shape themselves into audiences for specific texts offered by various media (Berger, 1995).

Companies are told that they need to use segmentation and targeting to reach their intended audience and to improve the chances that their message will be understood, because in the case of mass media such as advertisements, there is almost no feedback (Suchan & Dulek, 1988) and there is a disjunction of place and time between the communicator and reader (Bell, 1991) that can result in a delay or breakdown in the communication process. This forces advertisers who use print media, to note diligently who the reader is, the reader's knowledge level, position, motivation, biases, interest, demographics, unique characteristics, language ability and preference (Ober, 1995), the right stimuli (Gooding, 1998) and the correct cultural knowledge of the reader (McQuarrie & Mick, 1992; D. Mick & Buhl, 1992; Scott, 1990, 1994a; Stern, 1990) in order to get the right message across to the right person.

Segmentation

Market segmentation is a dominant, important and overriding concept in marketing theory and practice (Dickson, 1982). Segmentation was first discussed as being derived from the heterogeneity of customer wants (W. R. Smith, 1956), based on the theory of imperfect competition (Robinson, 1938). Market segmentation is described as the dissecting of a heterogeneous market into smaller homogeneous markets, in response to the differing preferences that can be attributed to the consumer's desire for more precise satisfaction of their wants (Kotler, 1997; Kotler & Armstrong, 1994; Kotler, Swee, Siew, & Chin, 1999; W. R. Smith, 1956). These markets are normally heterogeneous, culturally and socio-economically diverse (Douglas & Win, 1987; J. S. Hill & Still, 1984; Jain, 1989; Kale & Sudharshan, 1987; McKenna, 1992; Mehrotra, 1990) and therefore easily identified. Market segmentation is widely used as payoffs will be greater when a company matches its marketing mix to a particular segment (P. E. Green & Krieger, 1991; M. Wright, 1996).

The attraction of segmentation lies in the premise that the market can be divided into groups responsive to different marketing factors. Segmenting the market should allow the company to allocate its marketing resources more efficiently and effectively (Claycamp & Massy, 1968; Frank, Massy, & Wind, 1972) and build a loyal customer base (Kotler & Armstrong, 1994). This is achieved by differentiating the company's products and promotions to the needs of the different segments. Most companies have products that are differentiated. The success of segmentation is measured against several dimensions of successful segmentation (Frank et al., 1972; V. W. Mitchell, 1995; Wind, 1978).

Nevertheless, there are criticisms of segmentation. It is clearly noted that much of the associated research into segmentation and targeting has been superficial, normative and repetitive (Cooper & Lane, 1997; Hooley et al., 1998; Pinson & Jinnett, 1993). Segmentation has been criticized as difficult to implement due to the greater market diversity that exists now (Pingjun, 2000) and as not being workable (Kennedy & Ehrenberg, 2001).

The key assumptions of segmentation are also questioned. These include issues such as the bases for segmentation, variables used in segmenting markets and the number and composition of segments the company chooses to have (Esslemont & Ward, 1989; Hoek, Gendall, & Esslemont, 1996). Other academics have argued that if segmentation were successful, then there would be no need for targeting, as the choice would be obvious (M. J. Wright & Esslemont, 1994).

Ehrenberg and his colleagues have been among the most vocal critics of segmentation and targeting (Barnard & Ehrenberg, 1997; Collins, 1971; Ehrenberg, 1988, 1993, 2001; Ehrenberg et al., 1997; Ehrenberg & Goodhardt, 1978; Ehrenberg, Goodhardt, & Barwise, 1990; Hammond, Ehrenberg, & Goodhardt, 1995; Kennedy & Ehrenberg, 2001). Their research shows that the same people purchase products that are aimed at different segments, that there is low loyalty in various product classes and no particular choice of brand that will reduce the likelihood of purchases of other brands. This implies that marketers should use mass advertising, as there is no significant variation between people in their brand purchase behavior. In other words there are no loyal customers but customers who are polygamous in their choice of brand. This is

23

clearly in line with one of the propositions underlying this book which is, customers, when annoyed by specific ethnic group targeting may switch to other brands in their brand set.

Despite these arguments, there are still calls for segmentation and some empirical evidence that supports its use. Some authors still urge companies to segment their markets based on culture and ethnicity (Chudry & Pallister, 2002; Gitlin, 2001; Lawrence, Shapiro, & Lalji, 1986) even though there are conflicting findings (Lindridge & Dibb, 2003).

Targeting

Segmentation allows for targeting, which allows business's products, services, promotions and activities to be directed to a specific group chosen for the best possible outcome (Kotler & Armstrong, 1994). Targeting is the conscious choice of a segment while clearly neglecting other segments. By targeting, a company chooses a homogeneous group from the segmentation process to communicate with. Therefore there is a deliberate choice to exclude other groups who may still be exposed to the communication effort of the company.

The approach of targeted promotion is premised on the notion that communications are most effective when their elements refer to the targeted group culture (Hecht et al., 1993). These elements include the channel or medium used to transmit the information, the content of the message, the icons and symbols used to convey the message and values portrayed in the message. For example in Malaysia, Maybeline advertisements uses Siti Nurhaliza (a local singer) in their Malaysian advertisements whereas in America, advertisements that target African American uses RandB and hip-hop artists (Elkin, 1998). Advertisers know that in order to target and reach these groups, they must target them with a specific product (Y. K. Kim & Kang, 2001), appropriate language (Swift, 1991) understand the group's country of origin and its effect on the way they have seen/heard advertisements, as well as the length of time in a new country in the case of immigrants (Steere, 1995).

Targeted advertising is utilized in three ways; the first two are based on advertising stimuli and the third is founded on advertising effects. The first method customizes ad-content to the target market. In the second, advertisements are placed in varying degrees of intensity in different media. The third employs differential advertising effects and is usually assessed in laboratory settings (Ringold, 1995). Targeted advertising in this book works on the assumption that there is differentiation based on ethnicity, which allows for customization of advertisement content.

There have been a considerable number of empirical studies into the effects of targeting ethnic groups and their reactions to ethnically targeted advertisements. The findings suggest that ethnic self-awareness moderates consumer response to targeted advertising (Forehand & Deshpande, 2001) and is significant to how advertising is perceived (Shaffer & O'Hara, 1995) and purchased (Donthu & Cherian, 1994); (R. W. Pollay, Lee, & Carter-Whitney, 1992). Consumers also perceived advertisers differently based on the language they used in advertisements (Koslow et al., 1994). Differences in reactions by the dominant and non-dominant groups (either

24

numerically or culturally) have also been noted (Brumbaugh, 2002; Deshpande & Stayman, 1994; S. A. Grier & Deshpande, 2001; Tan & Farley, 1987). Other studies have noted that certain product categories lent themselves well to being targeted to ethnic groups, as they were more culturally sensitive (Webster, 1994). Nevertheless, the use of mass media to target ethnic groups has been questioned, as this is more suitable for a broad appeal rather than a targeted one (Schiffman & Kanuk, 1997).

There has also been some research into unsuccessful ethnic targeting advertisements. Problems included the target market feeling alienated as the advertisements were designed primarily for other ethnic groups or were adapted from advertisements that were successful for another ethnic group (Paul Herbig & Yelkur, 1998).

While segmentation and targeting appears to be important, much of the associated research has been superficial, normative and repetitive (Cooper & Lane, 1997; Hooley et al., 1998; Pinson & Jinnett, 1993). Some writers state that brand differentiation is unlikely and that advertisements cannot persuade but only reinforce (Barnard & Ehrenberg, 1997; Ehrenberg, 2001; Ehrenberg et al., 1997), which minimizes the possibility of effective targeting. Targeting also presupposes that a particular group is important (Barnard & Ehrenberg, 1997), while overlooking other groups. Nonetheless, segmentation, targeting and differentiation are the norm in the real world and are designed to obtain specific promotional effects. This does not imply that segmentation, targeting and differentiation should not be questioned. Instead, more critical research is needed.

The use of mass media as a vehicle for advertising may result in many different groups, aside from the targeted group, seeing the advertisement (R. W. Pollay, 1986) and reacting differently to it (Aaker et al., 2000; Brumbaugh, 2002; Csikszentmihalyi & Beattie, 1979; S. A. Grier & Brumbaugh, 1999; Whorf, 1941, 1956). This indicates a major weakness in segmentation, targeting and differentiation because, in theory, there should be no overlap between groups. Thus, Ehrenberg's arguments about the ineffectiveness of segmentation, targeting and differentiation (Ehrenberg et al., 1997; Ehrenberg & Goodhardt, 1978; Kennedy & Ehrenberg, 2001), consumers' multi-brand behavior and the lack of major difference in the characteristics of consumers who buy different brands (Barnard & Ehrenberg, 1997) provide support for a critical examination of the reactions of targeted and non-targeted advertising audiences.

Many targeting studies have noted the responses of the targeted group to the advertisement, brand, product or company, but a major flaw in the theory is that it does not note the unintended effects that may arise from non-target groups' reactions. Researchers have begun to note that marketers need to consider the non-target market (consumers who perceive themselves not to be the target of an advertisement) as well as the target market (S. A. Grier & Brumbaugh, 1999). This book intends to provide a comprehensive assessment of targeted and non-targeted groups' reactions to ethnically targeted advertisements and products as well as noting affective responses and reactions to the company behind the advertisements.

Intended and Unintended Effects of Advertising

Companies use various forms of mass communication based on the premise that there will be intended effects from the utilization of specific media. Nevertheless, questions have been raised about the strength, degree, incidence and type of effects that occur (D. McQuail, 1983). An effect is change (Piatila, 1977): 125) and there can be either intentional or unintentional changes.

Research into mass media effects has a long history. Initially, mass media communication was believed to have a very strong effect. The second phase was more cautious, with terms such as 'limited' used to describe the effects of mass media communication. The current thinking is more equivocal with effects and potential effects still being sought (Asp, 1986; De Fleur & Ball-Rokeach, 1982; D. McQuail, 1983; Windahl et al., 1992). Past research suggests that mass media communication effects are able to generate three major types of effect. The first involves the available stock of knowledge, values, opinions and culture. The second includes selection and response to the communication attempt. The third type entails socialization, reality definition, distribution of knowledge and social control (D. McQuail, 1983).

Other effects identified in mass media studies include change (Piatila, 1977), reinforcement of beliefs (Lazarfeld et al., 1944), enlargement effects (De Fleur & Ball-Rokeach, 1982), cognitive complexity effects (Pavlik, 1987), reciprocal effects (Lang & Lang, 1986), boomerang effect (Devito, 1986), spill-over effects (Lang & Lang, 1986), third-person effects (Davison, 1983), agenda setting effects (McCombs & Shaw, 1972) and cultivation effects (Gerbner et al., 1980).

Aside from noting the general effects of mass media communication, there is also a need to note the distinct effects of advertising. Advertisements are a form of message transference using mass media. Advertisements are designed professionally with a specific purpose of reinforcing certain behaviors and values (R. W. Pollay & Gallagher, 1990). The intended effects of an advertisement are specific, such as to influence the sales of products or services, or to influence variables that may be related to sales levels, such as brand image (Ottesen, 1981). Other intended effects include improved understanding of product and brand attributes, incentives to take action, reminders, and reinforcement of previous product and/or brand messages (Wells et al., 2002).

Advertising is a form of mass communication that allows for the possibility that anyone may see it (Barnard & Ehrenberg, 1997; R. W. Pollay, 1986). This appears to be a major difference between advertising and other forms of marketing communications, such as direct marketing, database marketing, or direct selling. Advertising utilizes mass media and therefore marketers cannot control who sees it, even if it is placed in specific targeted media (Cornwell, 1994; Ringold, 1995) creating the possibility of two types of unintended effects discussed earlier.

Studies of unintended effects of advertising are quite comprehensive and wide-ranging but tend to focus on social and moral issues. An extensive search of the literature reveals that unintended effects include inadequacy of women's self concepts (R. W. Pollay, 1986), reinforcing a preoccupation with physical attractiveness (Downs & Harrison, 1985; Gulas & McKeage, 2000; Myers & Biocca, 1992; Silverstein,

26

Perdue, Peterson, & Kelly, 1986) and determination of what constitute physical attractiveness (Martin & Kennedy, 1993; R. T. Peterson, 1987; Richins, 1991). Other critics of advertising have been harsher and argue that advertising encourages eating disorders (Gilly, 1999; R. T. Peterson, 1987) or that it compromises self esteem and financial success (Gulas & McKeage, 2000).

Other studies of unintended effects suggest that advertising might promote materialism (M. E. Goldberg & Gorn, 1978), status seeking, social stereotypes, short sightedness, selfishness, a preoccupation with sexuality and conformity (R. W. Pollay, 1986). Others have argued that the main unintended effects of advertisements are a narrow view of reality (Ottesen, 1981; R. W. Pollay, 1986; Richins, 1991, 1996), which affects values, taste and culture (Ottesen, 1981; R. W. Pollay, 1986). Children may be particularly vulnerable and may become less interested in social interactions, experience greater parent child conflict leading to a disappointed and unhappier child (M. E. Goldberg & Gorn, 1978).

From what has been discussed, it is clear that there are three main deficiencies in this field of study:

1.   Research mainly looks at the correlations between the degree of exposure to an advertisement and measured changes in experiences, acts, attitudes, opinions, or knowledge of those exposed to such media (Comstock, Chaffee, Katzman, McCombs, & Roberts, 1978; D. McQuail, 1983);
2.   Most studies of unintended effects focus on the consequences to the consumer and not the advertiser or the company;
3.   Most studies focus on social justice and moral issues.

Nevertheless these studies indicate that targeted advertising may generate unintended reactions from those that have been exposed to it, whether they are the targeted group or not. The challenge, then, is to determine whether targeted advertisements create unintended effects for a company, as a result of responses by those who are targeted and those who are not. The research model proposed in this book (refer to Figure 1), extends and adapts current research into social justice effects, to assess the marketing effects that targeted advertising may have on consumers and on the firm behind the advertising. The model could be used to assess intended and unintended effects, although the focus of this book is unintended effects.

Unintended Effects on the Company

An example of unintended effects on a company that uses targeted advertising may be a loss of sales to a competitor (Crain, 2002). Although examples on unintended company effects can be found, there is a dearth of empirical research. Nevertheless, it has been clearly shown in the earlier discussion of segmentation and targeting, that individuals not targeted will have their own meaning and reactions to the advertisement. Having said so, it is implied that these reactions will be negative (Brumbaugh, 2002; Feinberg et al., 2002; S. A. Grier & Brumbaugh, 1999; S. A. Grier & Deshpande, 2001; Holland & Gentry, 1999; Koslow et al., 1994; Touchstone et al., 1999). If this is so, then there is a need to assess whether the effects of targeted advertising on non-targeted groups, is significant enough to warrant companies taking precautionary measures when utilizing targeted advertising.

In order to do this, a number of factors need to be measured using explicit and validated scales: corporate credibility (Newell & Goldsmith, 2001); corporate image (Annan, 1999; Spencer, 1999); rapport (Crook & Booth, 1997); attitude towards the company (R. A. Peterson, Wilson, & Brown, 1992); positive word of mouth (WOM) (Becker & Kaldenberg, 2000); purchase intention (Maheswaran & Sternthal, 1990).

Other important reactions that need to be assessed include: attitude towards the advertisement (Henthorne, LaTour, & Nataraajan, 1993); attitude towards the brand (Gardner, 1985; Mitchel, 1986); attitude towards the product (Maheswaran & Sternthal, 1990); affective reactions (Touchstone et al., 1999). These measures are essential, because previous research into advertising effectiveness indicates that these are the main predictors of success (Jain, 1989; Koslow et al., 1994; Shoham, 1996; Touchstone et al., 1999).

3. CONCEPTUAL FRAMEWORK

Speech Accommodation Theory

Most models of communication are relatively simple and straightforward. The common elements in communication theories are the sender, message, receiver of the message and sometimes, a feedback loop (Burke, 1969; Corbett, 1965). The sender constructs his/her message according to his/her expectations of the receiver. The sender will utilize his/her body of knowledge, vocabulary and common experience to craft the message. Receivers of the message will also use the same body of cultural knowledge to read the message, infer the sender's intentions and evaluate the message. Thus cultural knowledge acts as the basis for normative interaction, which creates a feedback loop (Brumbaugh, 1995, 2002; McQuarrie & Mick, 1992; D. Mick & Buhl, 1992; Scott, 1990, 1994b; Stern, 1990).

Among the well-known models that deal with feedback is the Osgood-Schramm circular model (refer to Figure 2). It was amongst the initial models that broke away from the one way/linear model of communication (D. McQuail & Windahl, 1993). Other models include: Gerbner's model of communication; Jakobson's model of the communication process; Lasswell's communication model (Berger, 1995); the Static-Speech communication paradigm; and the Dynamic speech paradigm model (R. G. Smith, 1970). These models are concerned with the message, its transference and feedback between only two parties. As such, they do not look at the sender, except to superfluously note that he/she encodes and decodes the message. The message is paramount and neither the sender nor others who may view or hear the message are considered.

Figure 2 Osgood and Schramm's Circular Model

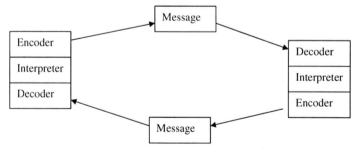

One exception is the SAT, which places importance on the sender and how the receiver of the message views the sender as well as the message. The two parts of this theory relate well with the focus of this book which is concerned with the actions of the message sender (the company) in trying to accommodate the receiver, as well as how the message receiver views the actions of the sender (H. Giles et al., 1973). This book extends the SAT to include how others outside the basic communication model view the sender of the targeted message (refer to Figure 1). Importantly, outcomes include corporate credibility, company image, attitude towards the company and rapport.

The SAT or, or as some have renamed it, the Communications Accommodation Theory or Accommodation Theory, has become quite popular in research in recent years. It has been used to research areas such as mass media (for example TV and radio) (Bell, 1991; Lipski, 1985; Montgomery, 1988; Roslow & Nicholls, 1996), print advertisements (Koslow et al., 1994), billboards (Touchstone et al., 1999), courts (Dixon, Tredoux, Durrheim, & Foster, 1994; Linell, 1991), medical consultation (Street Jr., 1991), mental disability (Hamilton, 1991), therapy (Ferrara, 1991), organizational communications (Bourhis, 1991), native interactions (Zuengler, 1991), ethnic accommodation (Gallois & Callan, 1991), gender (Bilous & Krauss, 1988; Fitzpatrick, Mulac, & Dindia, 1995; Mulac, Wiemann, Widenmann, & Gibson, 1988) and e-mail (Crook & Booth, 1997).

(H. Giles et al., 1973)) proposed the SAT (Figure 3) in a study that looked at how different language speakers tend to accommodate another language speaker when delivering a message. Initially, the theory leaned heavily on the Similarity-Attraction Theory (Byrne, 1969, 1971). The similarity-attraction theory states that the more similar our attitudes and beliefs are to a specific other, the more likely we will be attracted to them. Therefore early studies utilizing The Accommodation Theory predicted that "the greater the amount of effort in accommodation that a bilingual speaker of one group was perceived to put into his message, the more favorable he would be perceived by listeners from another ethnic group and also the more effort they in turn would put into accommodating back," (H. Giles et al., 1973: 177).

Figure 3 Speech Accommodation Theory

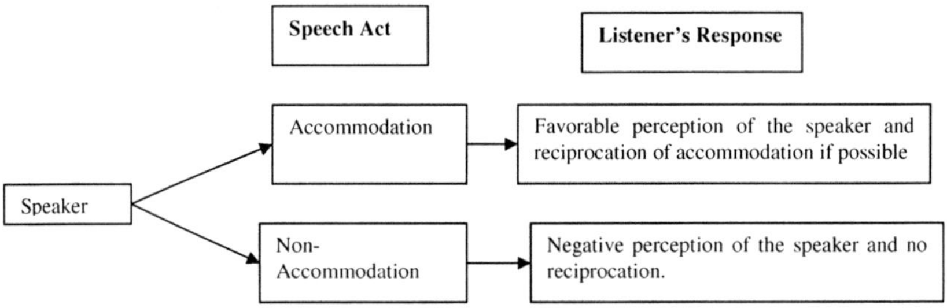

This theory has two parts. The first part involves the speaker who makes his/her style more similar to that of the audience. This process can include several methods including actual language shift (for example from Bahasa Malaysia to Iban), variations in pitch, speech rate, or response latency. This act is known as convergence and it is the act of accommodating the audience. This action is a strategy to integrate the audience with the speaker and to obtain a favorable response (H. Giles et al., 1973).

The second part of the theory involves the audience. It is too naïve to state that there is a direct relationship between an accommodating speaker and his/her audience response. Initially, this was posited (H. Giles et al., 1973), but as will be shown, there are optimal reactions (H. Giles & Smith, 1979), situational factors (Ball, Giles, Byrne, & Berechree, 1984), psychological and contextual factors (H. Giles, Coupland, & Coupland, 1991), motives and intentions (Simard, Taylor, & Giles, 1976) and incomplete or inappropriate convergence (J. Platt & Weber, 1984) that affect the response of the audience. If the audience thinks that there is too much accommodation, they may not accept it. An example would be the elderly, who find accommodated speech condescending and insulting (Coupland, Coupland, Giles, & Henwood, 1988).

When two speakers of different languages engage in conversation, they have to adjust their speech rate for each individual to accept the message/messenger as being more intimate and immediate (Buller & Anne, 1992). This is known as speech convergence or SAT in practice. Convergent strategies also occur when parties expect to interact more in the future (Walbott, 1995). If individuals are committed and dependent upon each other, it will encourage them to use accommodation strategies (Rusbult, Verette, Whitney, Slovik, & Lipkus, 1991).

The initial theory, however, was lacking in many respects, especially as it took no account of the receiver's knowledge of the sender's language skills, ability, intention, external pressure and effort. This was subsequently tested to note causal attribution in relation to the evoked emotions (Simard et al., 1976). The expanded theory utilized causal attribution processes to test accommodation theory (Heider, 1958; Jones & Davis, 1965; H. H. Kelly, 1973). The causal attribution processes suggest that we interpret other people's behavior and evaluate the person themselves, in terms of the motives and intentions that we attribute as the cause of their behavior. The Accommodation Theory was then revised and the results are depicted in Figure 4. This was further extended to include a situation where the speaker utilized incomplete or inappropriate convergence (refer to Figure 5) (J. Platt & Weber, 1984).

31

Figure 4 Simard's Version of the Accommodation Model

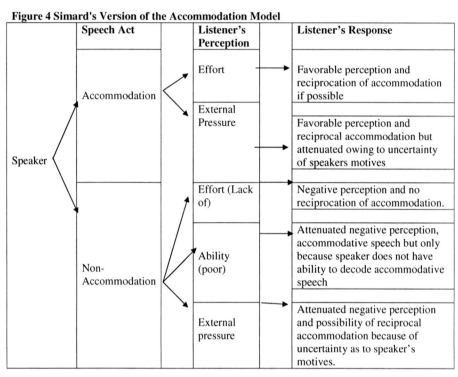

	Speech Act	Listener's Perception	Listener's Response
Speaker	Accommodation	Effort	Favorable perception and reciprocation of accommodation if possible
		External Pressure	Favorable perception and reciprocal accommodation but attenuated owing to uncertainty of speakers motives
	Non-Accommodation	Effort (Lack of)	Negative perception and no reciprocation of accommodation.
		Ability (poor)	Attenuated negative perception, accommodative speech but only because speaker does not have ability to decode accommodative speech
		External pressure	Attenuated negative perception and possibility of reciprocal accommodation because of uncertainty as to speaker's motives.

Figure 5 Platt And Weber's Revised Version of the Accommodation Model

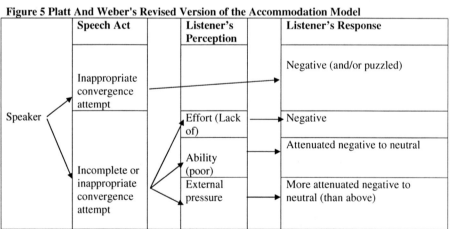

	Speech Act	Listener's Perception	Listener's Response
Speaker	Inappropriate convergence attempt		Negative (and/or puzzled)
	Incomplete or inappropriate convergence attempt	Effort (Lack of)	Negative
		Ability (poor)	Attenuated negative to neutral
		External pressure	More attenuated negative to neutral (than above)

Other factors that have been taken into consideration in the Accommodation Theory are the social exchange process (H. Giles & Smith, 1979; Homans, 1961) and processes of intergroup distinctiveness (Tajfel, 1974). The social exchange process refers to a situation where when one has the choice of doing A or B, one will tend to choose the alternative that maximizes the chances of a positive outcome and minimizes the chances of an unpleasant result. This can be linked to the Theory of Accommodation by the use of accents, where one tends to try to join one's speech to a perceived superior accent (H. Giles, 1971; H. Giles, Baker, & Fielding, 1975; H. Giles & Powesland, 1975). The processes of intergroup distinctiveness (Tajfel, 1974) propose that when members of different groups are in contact, they compare themselves on dimensions that are important to them. Individuals will then search for dimensions that will make them distinctive from others, which will create a specific social identity. Studies showed that speech style is an important subjective and objective clue to social group membership and therefore individuals will utilize speech as a way to make themselves distinctive from others (H. Giles, 1977a, 1977b; H. Giles, Bourhis, & Taylor, 1977; H. Giles, Taylor, Lambert, & Albert, 1976).

The Accommodation Theory is therefore an excellent basis for this research. It allows for the measurement of readers' reactions to both the company and its message. It has also been used in previous print advertising studies (Koslow et al., 1994) and allows for the use of language as a measure of accommodation. This ties in well with the current drive to target ethnic groups in advertising that utilizes the receivers' language (Koslow et al., 1994);(Cantwell, 2001; Hernandez & Newman, 1992; King, 1991; Lipski, 1985).

Language

Language is a group of arbitrary symbols possessing an agreed-upon significance within a specific community (Morris, 1946). These symbols have meaning because of agreement and convention. This means that there are groups of users who share important similar origins and segments of a common culture with a similar mode of communication. Language is more than just a tool for communication; it is also an emblem of groupness (Edwards, 1985) that allows for those in a specific group to understand intangible symbolic relevance, historical and cultural associations and the embedded cultural continuity (Steiner, 1975).

Ethnic groups such as the Malay, Chinese and Iban in Malaysia, have their own language and are at least bilingual. This is not uncommon as many, if not most, consumers in the world speak more than one language (Grossjean, 1982; Hoffman, 1991). Generally, there are two types of bilingualism: societal and individual.

Societal bilingualism is where, in a given society, two or more languages are spoken. There are three forms of societal bilingualism: the first is where two different groups and each of these groups are monolingual; the second is where all people in the society are bilingual; the third is where one group is monolingual and the other (normally the minority) is bilingual (Appleman & Muysken, 1987). Malaysians are mostly in the second group with a few in the third group.

The issue of bilingualism from an individual standpoint is also debated. One view is that an individual bilingual speaker must have native-like control of two or more languages (Bloomfield, 1933), while another view only requires some second language skills in one of the four modalities (speaking, listening, writing, reading)

(Macnamara, 1969). In the case of Malaysia, most people have quite strong control of two or more languages. However, studies have shown that individuals process advertisements better in their first language rather than their second (D. Luna & Peracchio, 2001) and have higher regard for the sensitivity of the advertiser when the advertisement is in their first language (Koslow et al., 1994).

Nevertheless, in the case of bilingual consumers their grasp and choice of language can range in a continuum, from one language to the other. Studies have noted that language in advertisements can also be on a continuum (Roslow & Nicholls, 1996). The use of any point along the continuum is viable for the company, though there may be different reader reactions due to different meanings about the company being conveyed and differences in the perceived importance of the customer to the company (Koslow et al., 1994; Mueller, 1992; Touchstone et al., 1999). Research experiments in the past have used five language conditions (Roslow & Nicholls, 1996) or a four-language mix in their advertisements (Koslow et al., 1994). In order to manipulate the language content in this research, a three level language mix was utilized. As an example, the three-level mix of language for Malay respondents could be Malay, Malay and Iban and solely Iban. This allows for the measurement of the accommodation attempt and reaction and limits the factorial design to a manageable size. Using a four or five level mix as used in previous studies would not be practical because of the large sample that would be required. Besides, it could be argued, use of a greater number of intermediate levels will not add more insight to the study.

Ethnicity, Ethnic Identification Strength and Acculturation

This section reviews the literature that forms the conceptual basis for various levels of targeting tested in the research model (refer to Figure 1). The three most relevant dimensions of ethnic targeting are ethnicity, ethnic identification strength and acculturation.

The identification of ethnicity allows for the development of an in-group measurement that is distinct and separate from other groups. Ethnicity and the related concepts discussed here allow for the determination of a specific group, distinct and separate from other groups, as well as assessing the strength of identification of each individual within the group.

Ethnicity is seen as crucial in examining and understanding the functioning and viability of most contemporary societies including multi-cultural societies like Malaysia (Abraham, 1999). Ethnicity refers to the way people are grouped together by their language, custom, religion, race and territory (UNRISD, 1999). In Malaysia, race (thus ethnicity for the government) is viewed as a biological concept, though most sociologists would disagree with this (Shanklin, 1993) and would argue that this is a social and political classification.

Malaysia may be a multi-ethnic nation, but it is quite clear that each ethnic group is distinct and separate from one another, much like a 'salad bowl' and not a 'melting pot.' This can be seen as consumers generally interact within their own group, prefer to speak their own language and identify themselves by their own ethnicity rather than by nationality (Abraham, 1999; Furnivall, 1948).

34

Ethnicity is both the appearance of homogeneity of a human population group and the belief of members of a population group that they belong to one another (Anonymous, 2001b). Ethnicity involves a common cultural heritage, a sense of peoplehood that is passed from one generation to another, a sense of belonging and the expression of cultural heritage (Renzetti & Curran, 1998). Another alternative is the view that ethnicity is a construction of identities, through social experiences (UNRISD, 1999). This sameness has a common thread in nearly all definitions of ethnicity, of either common origin or shared cultural traits (Hui, Laroche, & Kim, 1998). Ethnic groups are seen as a segment of a larger society whose members are thought, by themselves and/or by others, to have a similar origin and to share important segments of a common culture (Barth, 1969; Keyes, 1976; Vallee, 1982; Yinger, 1985).

This sense of peoplehood is a unifying factor, which leads to the fostering of ethnic pride and cohesiveness (Kitano, 1985). In Malaysia, there have been numerous attempts by the government to develop a national identity, which seeks to integrate the three major ethnic groups into one nation (Abraham, 1999; Chai, 1971; Federation of Malaya, 1956; Federation of Malaysia, 1985; Joseph & Holden, 2001). Ethnic divisions are obviously visible in Malaysia and are based on language use, in both formal and informal situations (Abraham, 1999).

Various authors have raised questions as to how ethnicity should be defined (Burton, 1996; Deshpande, Hoyer, & Donthu, 1986; Hui et al., 1998). Since (Weber, 1961) pioneering work on ethnicity, there has been much confusion over its constructs. It is agreed, at a basic level, in sociology and anthropology, that ethnicity is a concept that refers to the character or quality encompassing various indicators that are used to assign people to groups (Gordon, 1964). Ethnic origin is a de facto characteristic of a person and is constructed by various biological characteristics, such as skin color (Devos, 1975; Fishman, 1977a, 1977b; Penaloza, 1994). Ethnicity is more than just paternity, but also patrimony (the legacy of collectivity) and phenomenology (the meaning people attach to their descent as members of a collectivity) (Fishman, 1977a, 1977b). Nevertheless, this is quite different from ethnic identity, which utilizes a more subjective view. However, studies in DNA do not support a biological separation and indicate that there are no clear breaks delineating racial groups (Marshall, 1998).

Previous studies have utilized either one construct (M. Garcia & Lega, 1979); two constructs (Constantinou & Harvey, 1985); three constructs (Hogg, Abrams, & Patel, 1987); three or more (Aboud & Christian, 1979); or four or more constructs (Caltabiano, 1984; Driedger, 1975; Makabe, 1979) to determine ethnicity. Researchers have employed many methods to determine ethnicity such as surnames (Mirowsky & Ross, 1980), country of origin (Gurak & Fitzpatrick, 1982; Massey & Mulan, 1984), paternal ancestry (Alba & Moore, 1982), language spoken at home (Massey & Mulan, 1984), location of the city (Cervantes, 1980), area of residence (Wallendorf & Reilly, 1983) and self identification (Saegert, Hoover, & Hilger, 1985). The seven most widely accepted constructs of ethnic identity are language, friendship networks, religious affiliation, participation in clubs and organizations, endogamy, food preference and traditional celebrations (Driedger, 1975; Phinney, 1990; D. A. Rosenthal & Feldman, 1992).

There are two schools of thought regarding the definition of ethnicity. The first defines ethnicity through a subjective view, noting personal belief and an individual's own psychological identity about his/her cultural attributes (Laroche, Joy, Hui, & Kim, 1992), or a psychological phenomenon (Hraba, 1979). Ethnicity is more behavioral than race and therefore less rigid (Fishman, 1977b). Ethnicity can be seen through a person's acculturation process, is flexible, adaptable and takes different forms and meanings (Greeley, 1971; Isajiw, 1980) or a self-identity with a specific ethnicity (Reilly & Wallendorf, 1984).

The second more objective view of ethnicity looks at socio-cultural features such as religion, language, national origin, wealth, social status, political power, segregated neighborhoods and cultural tradition (Bennett, 1975; Burton, 1996; E. C. Hirschman, 1981; Keefe & Padilla, 1987). Nevertheless, it could be argued that even utilizing both subjective and objective views, it is still insufficient, as it does not measure the intensity of affiliation (Deshpande et al., 1986; E. C. Hirschman, 1981). This then brings us into the concept of 'ethnic identity' and 'ethnic identity strength.'

Ethnic identity is a concept that is answered by the questions "What am I?" and "What am I not?" (Aboud & Christian, 1979; Brand et al., 1974). It is a concept that refers to who a person is (Dashefsky & Shapiro, 1974; Frideres & Goldenberg, 1982) and is one of the many aspects in the identity of a person (Frideres & Goldenberg, 1982). The word identity conjures up many aspects that have to be considered, though in the case of this research, it must be limited to specific qualifiers of the word, 'ethnic' identity. Ethnic identity refers to one's identification to a specific ethnic group (Dashefsky & Shapiro, 1974; Driedger, 1978). In order for such identification to occur, a sense of common ancestry, based on shared individual characteristics or shared socio-cultural experiences (Driedger, 1978; Kitano, 1985), or a sense of shared values and attitudes (White & Burke, 1987), or feelings of belonging and/or commitment (Masuda, Matsumoto, & Meredith, 1970; Ting-Toomey, 1981), must exist. When this occurs, ethnic identity will tell a person the correctness of one's actions and at the same time allow for one to assess the correctness of an outsider's behavior (Frideres & Goldenberg, 1982). This is the reason respondents were asked for their reactions to a company that produced ethnically targeted advertising.

Ethnic identity can also be seen as the 'Japaneseness' (Masuda et al., 1970) or the 'Cubanness' (M. Garcia & Lega, 1979) of respondents. Studies have shown that ethnic identity has a significant influence on perceived in-group vitality (Gao, Schmidt, & Gudykunst, 1994). In this book, the 'Ibanness,' 'Malayness' and 'Chineseness' of respondents will be measured as a basis of identifying in-group vitality. The concept of ethnic identity allows for the incorporation of culture. It is a multidimensional construct (Christian, Gadfield, Giles, & Taylor, 1976; H. Giles et al., 1976) and the most widely accepted constructs of ethnic identity are used in this research.

Language has always been an important criterion in determining ethnic identity (Aboud & Christian, 1979; Bergier, 1986; Devos, 1975; Felix-Ortiz De La Garza, Newcomb, & Myers, 1995; H. Giles et al., 1976; Schermerhorn, 1970; Vallee, 1982). Most research measures also gauge media consumption (Bergier, 1986; M. Garcia & Lega, 1979; Keefe & Padilla, 1987) and the family context (Connor, 1977; Makabe, 1979; Masuda et al., 1970; Pierce, Clark, & Kaufman, 1978; Teske & Nelson, 1973;

Valencia, 1985). Language is important from the perspectives of proficiency, preference and use (Olmedo, 1979). Media consumption on the other hand can be seen as a private activity, determined by one's own choices and preferences and therefore will have little conflict with his/her own culture of origin (W. Lee & Tse, 1994b). Malaysian subcultures (i.e. Iban and Chinese) still use their ethnic languages even though they are fluent in the dominant language (Malay). This effect was also described for Hong Kong and Mexican migrants to the USA and Canada (W. Lee & Tse, 1994a; Penaloza, 1994). On the other hand, social use of language is more subject to the language of the dominant culture (Hui et al., 1998; W. Lee, 1993).

Other researches have utilized ethnic social interaction as a dimension for determining ethnic identity (Bergier, 1986; Connor, 1977; Dashefsky & Shapiro, 1974; Felix-Ortiz De La Garza et al., 1995; M. Garcia & Lega, 1979; Keefe & Padilla, 1987) while others have also noted the importance of religious affiliation (Dashefsky & Shapiro, 1974; E. C. Hirschman, 1981). Cultural aspects and cultural behavior had also been assessed (Hui et al., 1998).

Another way of determining ethnic identity is by ethnic self-labeling. It corroborates previous studies that state one can match one's own self identity with a specific ethnicity (Reilly & Wallendorf, 1984; Saegert et al., 1985). Ethnic self-labeling allows for the measurement of the degree of identification with an ethnicity (Deshpande et al., 1986; E. C. Hirschman, 1981) and has been used in numerous studies on Jewish ethnicity (E. C. Hirschman, 1981) as well as other studies for Hispanics (Deshpande et al., 1986; Saegert et al., 1985; Webster, 1994). Self-labeling is a subjective indicator of ethnicity and as such, a valid method of determining one's ethnicity. It is not uncommon for someone to speak and act as if they were in the main ethnic group but remain strongly psychologically attached to his or her group of origin (Penaloza, 1994).

Culture, on the other hand, is the part of human makeup that is learned by people as the result of belonging to a particular group (ethnic or otherwise) and it is that part of learned behavior that is shared by others (Kluckhohn, 1962). Culture is defined as "social settings in which a certain reference framework has taken concrete form or has been institutionalized and orients and structures the interaction and communication of people within this historical context" (Servaes, 1989):383). Culture is a distinct concept from ethnicity, where ethnicity is seen as involving paternity, patrimony (the legacy of collectivity) and phenomenology (the meaning people attach to their descent as members of a collectivity) (Fishman, 1977a, 1977b).

Societies have different ways of expressing culture. These differences are along the lines of power differences or social inequality, collectivism versus individualism, masculinity and femininity and uncertainty avoidance or control of aggression (Hofstede, 1991). Another view describes culture along the lines of individualism and collectivism (Triandis, 1994, 1995; Triandis, McCusker, & Hui, 1990). However, for the purpose of this book, culture is not an appropriate segmentation base.

Ethnic identity is a more appropriate segmentation base for this research because it is widely used in Malaysia though it has not been critically examined and is more likely to provide distinctive groups. However, it is apparent that ethnic identity can fade or be retained and be agreeable to change (Keefe & Padilla, 1987; Phinney, 1990). This fluidity is related to the concept of acculturation. For any marketer, an important issue in ethnicity is the strength of affiliation to a specific ethnicity and whether it has been diluted by the dominant culture, and if so, to what extent. This is known as acculturation, which is generally understood to be the acquisition or adoption of the host, main, or dominant cultural traits (Gentry, Jun, & Tansuhaj, 1995; Laroche, Kim, & Tomiuk, 1999; Laroche, Kirpalani, & Darmon, 1999), customs of an alternative society (Seitz, 1998), or a new culture (Andreasen, 1990; Hui et al., 1998).

Various models and schools of thought have described the process of acculturation. These include the linear bipolar model (Keefe & Padilla, 1987; Laroche, Kim et al., 1999; Olmedo, 1979; Phinney, 1990), complex model of acculturation (Berry, 1980; Goldlust & Richmond, 1977; Lambert & Taylor, 1990; W. Lee, 1993; Mendoza, 1989; Reilly & Wallendorf, 1984; Triandis, Kashima, Shimda, & Villareal, 1986; Yinger, 1985), the four stages of acculturation (Berry, 1990), the 150% man (McFee, 1968), or dimensions of change (Dohrenwend & Smith, 1962). These models all use similar constructs to measure acculturation.

Acculturation has been identified as a multidimensional construct (Keefe & Padilla, 1987; Mainous, 1989). Some acculturation researchers have even argued that their constructs are similar, if not the same as those for ethnicity (Phinney, 1990; Rogler, Cortes, & Malgady, 1991). The measures are similar, except that measures for ethnicity gauge the retention of the culture of origin and measures for acculturation determine the acquisition of a dominant culture. There are, however, a few studies that attempt the alternative proposition; to measure the acquisition of the host culture and the retention of culture of origin separately. Authors have reflected on the Cuban identity independently of a respondent's acquisition of the dominant (e.g. American) culture (M. Garcia & Lega, 1979). This method has resulted in typologies rather than summated scores, as for the linear bipolar model (Berry, 1980; Keefe & Padilla, 1987; Mendoza, 1989).

The most widely used acculturation construct is based on language (Burnam, Telles, Karno, Hough, & Escobar, 1987; Caetano, 1987; Cuellar, Harris, & Jasso, 1980; Franco, 1983; Olmedo, 1979; Rogler et al., 1991). Media type items are also commonly used (Caetano, 1987; M. Garcia & Lega, 1979; Huhr & Kim, 1984; Y. Y. Kim, 1977, 1978; Marin, Sabogal, Van Oss-Marin, Otero-Sabogal, & Perez-Stable, 1987; Triandis, Kashima, Hui, Lysansky, & Marin, 1982). Other major factors are social interaction and participation (Burnam et al., 1987; Caetano, 1987; Cuellar et al., 1980; Franco, 1983; Keefe & Padilla, 1987; Marin et al., 1987; Mendoza, 1989; Szapocznik, Kurtines, & Fernandez, 1980; Triandis et al., 1982), friends of the host culture and mass media preference (J. A. Garcia, 1982; Triandis et al., 1982; Weinstock, 1964). This is similar to the description earlier of the measurement scales used for ethnic identity.

However, in measuring acculturation one must note that there are two distinct caveats. The first is that it deals with individuals and therefore there is a presumption that individuals have considerable autonomy in which behavior to adopt from the dominant culture, which behavior to retain from their original culture and whether or not they want to do so (Burton, 1996). Constructs such as language and media usage can be thought of as private activities that are determined primarily by one's own choice (W. Lee & Tse, 1994b), though there may be structural constraints which force compliance (Wallendorf & Reilly, 1983).

A second caveat is that when the question of products or services is brought into the equation, there could be varying degrees of acculturation. Some consumption behaviors may be ingrained in an ethnic identity and therefore less likely to change regardless of the amount of time and interaction with the dominant culture. Others could change easily (W. Lee & Tse, 1994a).

Distinctiveness, In-Group Bias, Intergroup Bias Theory

The sense of oneness detailed in ethnicity definitions leads to the possibility of noting the distinctiveness of that oneness and identifying with it. The main hyporesearch of distinctiveness theory is that someone's distinct traits, in relation to others, will be more salient than the more common traits (McGuire, 1984; McGuire & McGuire, 1979, 1981). In the case of this book, it is proposed that the distinctiveness of Iban, in relation to Malay and Chinese, will be more salient than the common traits.

It has been argued that this salience is dominant when the group is a minority in terms of numbers (Deshpande & Stayman, 1994; Pollak & Niemann, 1998) while others argue for a social context to be taken into account (S. A. Grier & Deshpande, 2001; Moscovisi, 1975; Oakes, 1987; Tajfel, 1981). In the case of Iban, they are a minority group by number (Jabatan Perangkaan Malaysia Negeri Sarawak, 2002) but may be more similar to the Malay on certain social dimensions (Noriah, 1994; Postill, 1999; Tawai, 1997). Nevertheless, since their number is distinctly small and is limited to Sarawak, it was decided to use them as the targeted non-dominant group for this research.

Previous studies have shown that members of minority groups are more likely than majority groups to have salient ethnicity (Deshpande & Stayman, 1994). Because their distinctiveness has been singled out by targeted advertisements, consumers identify with the message source, trust the message source and have more favorable intentions towards the advertisement and the brand (Aaker et al., 2000; Deshpande & Stayman, 1994; Forehand & Deshpande, 2001; S. A. Grier & Brumbaugh, 1999; Jensen, 1998; Mehra, Kilduff, & Brass, 1998).

However, the distinctiveness theory does not describe how other groups are likely to react to the group being targeted. The in-group and intergroup bias theory helps to explain this. The in-group bias theory suggests that bias towards one's own group represents favoritism, but does not imply disfavor towards other groups (M.B. Brewer, 1979). The attachment to one's in-groups does not necessarily require hostility towards out-groups (Allport, 1954; M. B. Brewer, 1999). Studies have shown that in-group identification is independent of negative attitudes towards out-groups and that much in-group bias and intergroup discrimination is motivated by preferential treatment of in-group members rather than direct hostility toward out-group members (M. B. Brewer, 1999). It is the emotional responses (prejudice) that creates hostility towards out-groups.

Intergroup bias refers to the tendency to evaluate one's own membership group (the in-group) more favorably than a non-membership group (the out-group) (Hewstone, Rubin, & Willis, 2002). This is reflected by specific behaviors such as discrimination, prejudice (emotional reaction), or stereotyping (cognitive reaction) (Mackie & Smith, 1998). Intergroup bias is concerned with the tendency to favor the in-group and disfavor the out-group and is seen as a general phenomenon (Hagendoorn, 1993, 1995; Verkuyten, Hagendoorn, & Masson, 1996).

By categorizing oneself as part of a specific group, one assimilates one's self to the in-group (Brown & Gaertner, 2001) and the group is cognitively tied in with the self (E. R. Smith & Henry, 1996). This allows for the building of trust, positive regards, cooperation and empathy with those in the in-group (M. B. Brewer, 1999, 2001; Insko, Schopler, Hoyle, Dardis, & Graetz, 1990). The bias that occurs is in the form of in-group favoritism (M. B. Brewer, 1999; Hewstone et al., 2002) rather than an all out derogation of the out-group. However, this may dissipate when the out-groups are associated with stronger emotions such as fear, hatred, disgust or intergroup encounters that create such emotions (Doosje, Branscombe, Spears, & Manstead, 1998; Mackie & Smith, 1998; E. R. Smith, 1993; Stephan & Stephan, 2000).

Therefore in this book, each ethnic group would be expected to evaluate advertisements that use their own language more preferably than advertisements that use another group's language. The use of ethnicity and ethnic identification strength will allow for a determination of which group the respondents perceive themselves to be in. This is manipulated in the study by the different advertisements. It is therefore expected that one would react positively to an advertisement in one's own language because of favoritism to one's own group. Any strong negative reactions would be because of emotional response (prejudices) towards the other group rather than a cognitive appraisal of the advertisement. Because the targeted advertisements are essentially an out-group advertisement, that is distinctively different, the reactions to such advertisements are likely to be negative.

Social Distance

Social distance is a concept that measures the distance between identified ethnic groups. (Bogardus, 1925) introduced the social distance scale for use as an index of the social distance that respondents perceive between themselves and members of different groups defined by nationality, ethnicity, religion, or politics.

The scale, or some form of it, has been used in studies involving a variety of populations, including ethnic minorities (Bogardus, 1967; Fagan & O'Neill, 1965; P. R. Kunz & Oheneba-Sakyi, 1989; Lambert & Taylor, 1990; Payne Jr., York, & Fagan, 1974), majority group members (Weiner, 1974) and occupational groups (Elliot, Hanzlik, & Gliner, 1992).

It has also been used to measure prejudice and distance between the main culture to Black, Hispanic, Jewish and Asian cultural groups in the USA (Hraba, Radloff, & Gray-Ray, 1999; Raden, 1998; Wilson, 1996) and has been adapted to measure distance between prisoners and those that work with them (Camp, Saylor, & Wright, 2001; Schram, 1999), the perception of the people towards deviants (J. Kunz & Kunz,

2001), models (Prabu, Morrison, Johnson, & Ross, 2002), patients with mental illness (Corrigan, Edwards, Green, Diwan, & Penn, 2001; Link, Phelan, Bresnahan, Stueve, & Pescosolido, 1999), friends (Krackhardt & Kilduff, 1999), foreigners becoming citizens (Walsh, 1990), tourists (Baum, 1996), shops (Dicson & MacLachlan, 1990) and healthcare providers (Malat, 2001).

The social distance scale is not without its detractors. It is a scale created from the perspective of the dominant group (M. Y. Lee, Sapp, & Ray, 1996) and its averaging process used to select the response categories ignores individual differences in the rank ordering of the categories, focusing instead on the order of the group means (Bjerke & Al-Meer, 1993). Another issue is cross-cultural transferability of the scale, as it was developed in a culture where people use a particular hierarchy of relationships associated with the high individualism and individual mobility characteristics of Western societies (Hsu, 1983; Triandis, 1995). In non-Western societies, which are typically more collectivist, this hierarchy may not exist or may be present in some other form (Weinfurt & Moghaddam, 2001). Nevertheless it has been replicated with similar findings but with smaller distance values and more homogeneity (Klegg & Yamamoto, 1998).

Researchers using this concept have found that social distance leads to territoriality (Lyman, 1995; Raden, 1998), interaction issues (those who are socially distant have little interaction) (Akerlof, 1997) and intergroup differentiation in communication patterns in multiple types of communication networks with the in-group and out-group members (Suzuki, 1998). Similarity to self and ethnic hierarchy was significantly the stronger predictor in social distance (Verkuyten & Kinket, 2000; Worthen, McGlynn, Solis, & Coats, 2002) and it has been used in intergroup alliances to hinder another group (Brinkerhoff & Jacob, 1994).

Other findings indicate that people tend to perceive relations close to and distant from themselves as more balanced than relations of intermediate distance (Krackhardt & Kilduff, 1999). This is clear in findings where both Blacks and Mexican Americans were more accepting of contact with Anglos than of contact with each other (Dyer, Vedlitz, & Worchel, 1989). Other studies found that ethnicity influences the desire for social distance even when socioeconomic characteristics are explicitly controlled (Schwartz & Link, 1991). This clearly indicates that social distance can be utilized in the model as a measurement of differences between ethnic groups.

Dominant and Non-Dominant Ethnic Groups' Reactions to Targeted Advertisements

The issue of dominance has only been discussed in the social sciences literature relatively recently. The social dominance theory proposes that society contains ideologies that encourage or moderate intergroup hierarchies (Sidanius & Pratto, 1999), which allows for a hierarchical society. How such dominant and non-dominant groups socialize is depicted in studies of cultural schemas (Brumbaugh, 1995, 2002; S. A. Grier & Brumbaugh, 1999).

It has been shown in previous research that members of a dominant cultural group are socialized into one culture (the dominant culture) and therefore have only one set of cultural models that may be activated and acted on (stored in dominant cultural models) (Brumbaugh, 2002). Therefore, the judgment of the dominant ethnic group towards advertisements is colored by their own cultural models, which may be internalized differently by individuals, yet similar overall (Quinn, 1992). These models are used to determine their opinions of advertisements targeted at them or to other groups. Knowledge of a subculture may be a sociotype (Triandis, 1994) or a stereotype (Katz & Braly, 1933). Stereotype refers to cognitive heuristics that are used when there is low motivation (Bargh, 1990; Kruglanski, 1990) and is believed to bias information by means of selective attention and recall (Johnson & Sherman, 1990). Non-dominant groups on the other hand, are socialized into both their culture and the dominant culture (Brumbaugh, 1995). Therefore both their own schema and the dominant schema affects how a non-dominant group reacts to an advertisement.

It is clear that most advertisements utilize the dominant ethnic group cultural cues (i.e. a "standard" advertisement) and therefore the dominant ethnic group will process the advertisement easily based on their cultural model. However, if the advertisement is different and is seen as targeting other groups (i.e. a "novel" advertisement), the dominant ethnic group will process these advertisements based on their knowledge of the subculture. The non-dominant group, on the other hand, will process it based on the number and strength of the schemas they have.

The Influence of Culture

One major factor that may add to the reader reciprocating favorably or unfavorably to targeted advertisements is culture. Culture has been described as "the social settings in which a certain reference framework has taken concrete form or has been institutionalized and orients and structures the interaction and communication of people within this historical context" (Servaes, 1989):383. It has been noted that culture includes beliefs, values and norms (Resnick, 1991) shared by the group and that it has been passed down from one generation to another (historical context). These frameworks are also known as schemas (M. S. Roth & Moorman, 1988) or cultural models (Quinn & Holland, 1987). They are only passed down to the group and non-members do not know them. Thus, culture defines groups of people and these reference frameworks create the context in which the message is seen, understood and reciprocated. As such, a Malay viewer would be expected to respond to an advertisement differently from an Iban or a Chinese viewer and vice versa.

It has been shown that when a cue is regularly connected to a cultural group, it will then be more strongly linked to that group and would more easily activate cultural models associated with the group. Source cues such as skin color and facial structure are highly salient and are processed quickly and automatically (Greenwald & Banaji, 1995; Macrae & Bodenhausen, 2000) compared to other advertising cues (Petty & Cacioppo, 1981). However, if the cues used are non-source cues such as background setting and language, which may not be as visually salient as source cues, it may require more processing or not processed at all (Chaiken & Maheswaran, 1994). However if the associative strength between the non-source cue and cultural model is strong, these cues will still activate thought and response.

4. RESEARCH DESIGN AND MAIN STUDY

Research Propositions

Targeting

The propositions in this area aim to test how those not targeted react to a targeted advertisement. Of key interest in this book is of whether there are any differences in emotions, attitude to the advertisement, attitude to the company and behavioral intentions, from those not targeted as compared to those targeted. This is achieved by presenting respondents with an advertisement that has been controlled for its ethnic background with the only difference between the various advertisements shown is the language used.

The different languages and mixture of languages in the advertisements reflect the levels of accommodation or targeting. The fully accommodated advertisement is the advertisement with the Iban background and Iban language only. All other advertisements have the same background but differ in the language used. They are seen as accommodating various ethnic groups and to varying levels, depending on the language mix (e.g. Iban only, mixture of Iban and Malay, Malay only).

Previous studies have shown that the reaction of those targeted is generally positive. Studies have also shown that respondents prefer their own language in an advertisement and process it better (Gerritsen et al., 2000; Koslow et al., 1994; D. Luna & Peracchio, 2001). Nevertheless, it is also widely held that those not targeted are potentially able to see a targeted advertisement (Barnard & Ehrenberg, 1997; R. W. Pollay, 1986). It is clear that those not targeted construct various meanings about the advertisement as well as the company (Csikszentmihalyi & Beattie, 1979; Whorf, 1941, 1956) and may react negatively to the company and its promotional activity.

As a result, several propositions were tested. Firstly, ethnic groups not targeted will have more negative emotional reactions than those targeted. Also, they will show more negative attitudes toward the advertisement than those targeted and have more negative attitudes toward the company than those targeted. Fourthly, ethnic groups not targeted will be less likely to purchase the product than those targeted and lastly, ethnic groups not targeted will be less likely to recommend the product than those targeted.

Accommodation

The accommodation theory states that that the greater the amount of effort in accommodation, the more favorable the reaction (H. Giles et al., 1973). The various levels of accommodation are achieved by using language as a method of accommodating a specific group, thus incorporating the distinctiveness and oneness of the group into the experiment (Edwards, 1985; Steiner, 1975). In order to depict accommodation, this research utilized language at three different levels on a continuum (Roslow & Nicholls, 1996).

An accommodated advertisement refers to an advertisement that is seen as targeting a specific group, i.e. Malay language advertisement for Malay respondents. A partially accommodated advertisement refers to an advertisement that is seen as incorporating another groups' language into the advertisement. In this case, the Malay language was used, creating a Malay/Iban language advertisement. A non-accommodating advertisement is an advertisement that is accommodating to another group. In this study, an advertisement using solely Iban language seen by Malay respondents was used.

The use of language is based on previous studies that show language to be an emblem of groupness (Edwards, 1985). Language allows for those in a specific group to understand the cultural model being depicted (Steiner, 1975) and create their own meaning based on their cultural schema (Aaker et al., 2000; Brumbaugh, 2002; Csikszentmihalyi & Beattie, 1979; S. A. Grier & Brumbaugh, 1999; Whorf, 1941, 1956). Studies have also shown that individuals process advertisements better in their first language than their second (D. Luna & Peracchio, 2001) and therefore would score higher for advertisements in their own language. Their preference and reaction would be less for the "middle ground" advertisement and most negative for advertisements not accommodating them.

With this in mind, the following propositions were made. Firstly, the more the target group is accommodated, the stronger the non-target groups' negative emotional reactions will be. Next, the more the target group is accommodated, the stronger the non-target groups' negative attitude towards the advertisement will be. Also, the more the target group is accommodated, the stronger the non-target groups' negative attitude towards the company will be and the non-targeted groups' intention to purchase will be less. Lastly, the more the target group is accommodated, the less the non-targeted groups' will positively recommend the product.

Dominant and Non-Dominant Ethnic Groups' Reactions to Novel and Standard Advertisements
It has been shown that the dominant ethnic group use only its cultural schema by which it base judgments of all other groups (Aaker et al., 2000; Brumbaugh, 2002; S. A. Grier & Brumbaugh, 1999). The dominant ethnic group will process standard advertisements (with expected language and usual cues) easily based on their cultural model. Novel advertisements (with uncommon or unexpected language and cues) will be taken notice of and processed based on the dominant ethnic group's knowledge of the subculture, be it either a sociotype or stereotype.

A standard advertisement refers to an advertisement with an Iban background and Malay language. Two different novel advertisements are used: the first has an Iban background and Iban language; the second, an Iban background and Chinese language. Although Malaysian viewers could expect to see standard advertisements, they would not expect to see novel advertisements used extensively. The latter has been designed to incorporate cues that are pertinent to the Iban (background, language) or Chinese (language), that when seen by the dominant group, will be noticed and processed.

This leads us then to the following propositions. Firstly, the dominant ethnic group will have a more negative emotional reaction to the novel advertisement than a

44

standard advertisement. Next, the dominant ethnic group will have a more negative attitude towards the novel advertisement than a standard advertisement. Also, the dominant ethnic group will have a more negative attitude to the company when the advertisement is novel compared with a standard advertisement and will be less likely to buy the product after viewing the novel advertisement compared with a standard advertisement. Finally, it is proposed that the dominant ethnic group will be less likely to recommend the product depicted in the novel advertisement than the standard advertisement.

Non-dominant ethnic groups share the same schema as the dominant ethnic group but they also have an alternative subcultural model that is coupled to their cognitive representations of self (Aaker et al., 2000; Brumbaugh, 2002; S. A. Grier & Brumbaugh, 1999). This creates a divergent tension that is resolved by either following the dominant group's lead or staying true to his or her own cultural schema.

The first part of the proposition is based on the view that a non-dominant group will have the cultural schema of the dominant group as well as their own (Brumbaugh, 2002). Therefore the non-dominant group will react as the dominant group when it views a novel advertisement that is not culturally relevant to them. However, when the non-dominant group sees a novel advertisement that is culturally relevant to them, they should employ their own schema in reacting to it. Therefore this leads to the following propositions. Firstly, the non-dominant ethnic group will have a more negative emotional reaction when viewing a novel advertisement that is not related to their cultural schema compared to a standard advertisement. Also, the non-dominant ethnic group will have a more positive emotional reaction when viewing a novel advertisement that is related to their cultural schema compared to a standard advertisement. Thirdly, the non-dominant ethnic group will have a more negative attitude to the advertisement when the advertisement is novel and not related to their cultural schema compared to a standard advertisement.

The non-dominant ethnic group will also have a more positive attitude to the advertisement when the advertisement is novel and related to their cultural schema compared to a standard advertisement, will have a more negative attitude to the company when the advertisement is novel and not related to their cultural schema compared to a standard advertisement and will have a more positive attitude to the company when the advertisement is novel and related to their cultural schema compared to a standard advertisement. It is also proposed that the non-dominant ethnic group will be less likely to purchase the product after viewing a novel advertisement that is not related to their cultural schema compared to a standard advertisement but will be more likely to purchase the product after viewing a novel advertisement that is related to their cultural schema compared to a standard advertisement.

The non-dominant ethnic group will be less likely to recommend the product after viewing a novel advertisement that is not related to their cultural schema compared to a standard advertisement and lastly, it is proposed that the non-dominant ethnic group will be more likely to recommend the product after viewing a novel advertisement that is related to their cultural schema compared to a standard advertisement.

Within Group Differences

Ethnic identity is a concept that is answered by the questions "What am I?" and "What am I not?" (Aboud & Christian, 1979; Brand et al., 1974). By noting the strength of this identification, it becomes a measurement for in-group distance (Gao et al., 1994). Studies have shown that the stronger a person identifies with his/her group, the stronger their reactions are (Deshpande et al., 1986). If they are not targeted, their reactions are likely to be more negative than weak ethnic group identifiers. This then leads to the following propositions.

Strong ethnic group identifiers that were not targeted by the fully or partially accommodated advertisements will have more negative emotional reactions than weak identifiers, will have more negative attitudes towards the advertisement than weak identifiers and will have more negative attitudes towards the company than weak identifiers. Also, strong ethnic group identifiers that were not targeted by the fully or partially accommodated advertisements will be less likely to purchase the product than weak identifiers and will be less likely to recommend the product than weak identifiers.

Between Group Differences

Social distance is a concept that measures the perception of the majority towards their distance to ethnic minorities (Bogardus, 1967). It depicts territoriality (Lyman, 1995) and amount of interaction (Akerlof, 1997). As such, it is used in my model as a measurement of distance between the non-targeted groups to the targeted group. The greater the distance between these groups, the stronger their reactions are likely to be towards advertisements that target another group.

With this in mind, the folowing propositions have been made. Firstly, strong social distance group identifiers that were not targeted by the fully or partially accommodated advertisements will have more negative emotional reactions than weak social distance group identifiers. Secondly, they will have more negative attitude to the advertisement than weak social distance group identifiers. Also, they will have more negative attitude to the company than weak social distance group identifiers and will be less likely to purchase the product than weak social distance group identifiers. Lastly, strong social distance group identifiers that were not targeted by the fully or partially accommodated advertisements will be less likely to recommend the product than weak social distance group identifiers.

Preliminary Design and Pre-test

In the preliminary stage, two decisions had to be made; the choice of product to be used in the experiment and the design of the advertisement. The choice of product – a fictitious brand of soft drink - was decided as a result of a brainstorming session. The product had to have broad appeal and be part of a product category that is frequently advertised in the mass media in Malaysia. A professional advertisement designer in Sarawak, Malaysia, designed the advertisement.

In the pre-test stage, four pretests were conducted to choose the advertisement design, determine that it was seen as targeting the correct group, test social distance scale and to determine that the translation and format of the questionnaire were acceptable to the target reader.

Main Study

In the main study, three factorial designs were employed. Factorial designs have been used in similar studies in advertising by other authors (Clarke, 1984; M. E. Goldberg & Gorn, 1974). The use of a factorial design was determined by the question at hand, propositions and treatments required. A factorial design allows for the use of more than one factor, simultaneously, by forming groups of all possible combinations of the values of the various variables used (Hair Jr., Anderson, Tatham, & Black, 1998; McAlister, Straus, Sackett, & Altman, 2003).

The first was a 5 (Advertisement Type: Iban; Malay; Chinese; Malay and Iban; Malay and Chinese) X 3 (Ethnic Group: Iban; Malay; Chinese) factor design to note the impact of ethnicity. The second was a 5 (Advertisement Type: Iban; Malay; Chinese; Malay and Iban; Malay and Chinese) X 3 (Ethnic Group: Iban; Malay; Chinese) X 2 (Ethnic Identification Strength: High; Low) factor design to note the impact of ethnic identification strength. The third was a 5 (Advertisement Type: Iban; Malay; Chinese; Malay and Iban; Malay and Chinese) X 3 (Ethnic Group: Iban; Malay; Chinese) X 2 (Social Distance: High; Low) factor design to note the impact of social distance.

These factorial designs were based on the research question, initial model (refer to Figure 1) and propositions discussed in Chapter Three. Interaction effects were tested by MANOVA and GLM, with a post hoc test utilizing Tukey's test. The propositions were tested using t-test with a Bonferroni Corrections Test.

Data Collection - Respondents and Sampling Process
The decision concerning sample size was predetermined by the considerations of the factorial design used. A minimum of 50 respondents per cell meant that there was a requirement of 250 respondents' per ethnic group. A breakdown of the number of respondents obtained per advertisement type is detailed in Table 1 and details about respondents' profiles are presented in Table 2. A total of 1173 respondents from Sarawak, Malaysia, were used in the main study consisting of 376 Iban, 405 Malay and 392 Chinese respondents.

Table 1 Advertisements Used in Main Study and Breakdown by Ethnicity

Background	Language	Number Of Respondents		
		Iban	Malay	Chinese
Iban	Iban	75	77	76
Iban	Malay	76	82	79
Iban	Chinese	75	80	83
Iban	Malay / Iban	75	76	77
Iban	Malay / Chinese	75	90	77

Table 2 Respondent Profiles

Factor		Popula-tion* (%)	Sample			
			Overall	Iban	Malay	Chinese
N			1173	376	405	392
Gender (%)	Male	51	40.6	47.3	32.3	42.6
	Female	49	59.4	52.7	67.7	57.4
Age Scale (%)	17 – 19	9	6.6	9.6	2.5	7.9
	20 –29	16	47.1	46.8	44.9	49.7
	30 – 39	15	29.2	26.1	34.3	27.0
	40 – 49	12	14.3	14.1	15.6	13.3
	50 – 59	8	2.5	2.7	2.7	2.0
	60 – 69	4	.3	.8	0	0
Highest Level Of Education Achieved (%)	No Formal Education		1.7	3.5	1.2	.5
	Primary School		5.4	10.6	5.2	.5
	Secondary School		68.4	68.1	75.6	61.2
	Diploma		16.3	10.9	14.3	23.5
	Degree		7.7	6.1	3.5	13.5
	Postgraduate		.6	.8	.2	.8
Stated Ethnicity (%)	Iban		32.1	100	0	0
	Malay		34.5	0	100	0
	Chinese		33.4	0	0	100
Ethnic Identification (%)	1		-	1.1	.5	.5
	2		-	3.2	.5	2.8
	3		-	9.6	5.9	11.0
	4		-	13.6	13.6	16.3
	5		-	19.1	20.7	30.4
	6		-	26.1	35.1	29.1
	7		-	27.4	23.7	9.9
Social Distance (%)	Marry		-	-	34.5	16.3
	Close friends		-	-	31.3	26.0
	Close neighbors		-	-	5.0	9.2
	Someone to talk to		-	-	9.9	31.4
	Office mate		-	-	18.9	15.8
	Visitor to my country		-	-	.2	.8
	Not allowed into my country		-	-	.2	.5

* Source: (Jabatan Perangkaan Malaysia Negeri Sarawak, 2003)

The population from which the sample was sourced was persons in Sarawak, Malaysia, that identified themselves as Malay, Iban or Chinese at the time of the study. Convenience sampling was utilized with individual subjects representing individual sampling units. This method has been suggested as satisfactory for theory-testing purposes (Mittal, 1995).

In order to obtain the required number of respondents, assistance was obtained from the Ministry of Unity, Sarawak, Malaysia. Most of the questionnaires (1000 copies) were distributed via the Ministry of Unity to its 'Tabika Perpaduan' program teachers. The Ministry official in charge was informed of the data gathering procedure and the questionnaire was explained in detail to him. The questionnaire was then distributed throughout Sarawak and was collected two months later.

Only 800 questionnaires were returned due to refusal and lack of time. The author and other enumerators distributed the remaining portion of the questionnaire (200 copies) plus extra 380 copies at various locations in Kuching, Sarawak. The final response rate was 74% where 1173 was the total number of questionnaires collected (800 copies in the first batch and 373 copies in the second batch) and another 1580 which consist of the initial distribution plus the total number of questionnaires sent out the second time (580 copies).

Respondents were selected on the basis of opportunity and availability. The interviewer approached them at their homes or offices. In cases where it was uncertain whether the respondents belonged to one of the ethnic groups in the study, they were asked to indicate their ethnicity. If they were not of the ethnic group studied, the author or enumerator then thanked them and left. If the respondent qualified, they were then greeted and asked if they were willing to be interviewed or to answer the questionnaire. Most respondents in the first phase of the data collection read and answered the questionnaire privately. Others, especially the older respondents and those met at the various villages in the second phase of data collection, preferred the questionnaire to be read to them by the enumerator and they indicated their answers. The subjects were told that the study was being carried out as a part of the author's research requirement and that the purpose of the study was to note their views of the advertisement before them.

Non-Response Bias Checks
As noted previously, non-response bias was checked by both a field and office edit (Churchill Jr., 1983). As in any survey method, there will be non-response. The initial non-response from the survey carried out by the Ministry of Unity was deemed as acceptable as the final calculated response rate was high (74%) (Churchill Jr., 1987). The main reason given for non-response was refusal to answer the survey and the lack of time for enumerators to obtain response. A total of 201 questionnaires were found to contain some form of item omission. This was initially coded in as '0' in the first coding in SPSS.

49

Table 3 Summary of Sources of Key Measurement Scales

Measure	Author	No. Of Items	Scale Range	No. Of Factors	Reliability	Validity	Scale Type
Corporate Credibility	(Newell & Goldsmith, 2001)	8	1 - 7	2	0.77 To 0.91	Yes*	L+
Corporate Image	(Annan, 1999)	22	1 - 5	6	0.70 To 0.88	Yes**	B++
	(Spencer, 1999)	14	1 – 5	3	0.87	Yes**	L
Rapport	(Crook & Booth, 1997)	14	1 - 7	1	0.96	Yes**	L
Attitude Toward The Company In The Advertisement	(R. A. Peterson et al., 1992)	3	1 - 5	-	0.91	No	B
	(Simard et al., 1976)	2	-	-	-	-	-
Attitude Toward Advertisement	(Henthorne et al., 1993)	6	1 - 4	-	0.77	No	B
Affect Towards The Advertisement	(Walker & Dubitsky, 1994)	1	1 - 5	-	-	No	L
Attitude Towards Brand	(Gardner, 1985; A. A. Mitchell & Olson, 1981)	4	1 - 7	-	0.93	No	B
Attitude Towards Product	(Maheswaran & Sternthal, 1990)	7	1 - 7	1	0.81	Yes**	B
Purchase Intention	(Maheswaran & Sternthal, 1990)	1	1 - 7	-	-	No	L
Word Of Mouth	(Becker & Kaldenberg, 2000)	1	1 - 5	-	-	No	L
Emotion – Alienation	(Touchstone et al., 1999)	2	1 - 9	-	0.6#	No	L
Anger		3			0.74		
Racism		2			0.47#		
Target Of The Advertisement		3			0.51		
Threatened By The Advertisement		3			0.73		
Advertiser's Sensitivity	(Koslow et al., 1994)	2	-	-	0.749#	Yes**	-
Social Distance	(Bogardus, 1925)	7	-	-	-		
Strength Of Ethnic Identification	(Donthu & Cherian, 1994)	4	1 - 5	-	0.79	No	L
	(Deshpande et al., 1986)	1	1 - 5	-	-	No	L
	(Appiah, 2001)	5	1 - 7	-	0.87	No	L

* = Exploratory and Confirmatory Factor Analysis, ** = Exploratory Factor Analysis, + = Likert Scale, ++ = Bi-polar Scale, # = Pearson correlations coefficient alpha.

There are three methods to deal with item omission. The first is to treat the missing data as a separate category, the second is to conduct a multiple regression to determine the missing values and the third is to calculate a figure based on the average for that item (Churchill Jr., 1987). The third option was chosen and carried out on all the missing items.

Reliability Evaluation
Reliability refers to the similarity of results provided by independent but comparable measures of the same object, trait, or construct (Churchill Jr., 1987). A similar

definition, noting the amount of agreement between independent attempts to measure the same theoretical concept, was proposed by (Bagozzi, 1994). In essence, it is a method that describes the degree to which observations or measures are consistent or stable (R. Rosenthal & Rosnow, 1991) or accurate and precise (Thorndike, Cunningham, Thorndike, & Hagen, 1991).

Reliability was assessed based on Cronbach Alpha as presented in Tables 10 and 11. The Cronbach Alpha reflects both the number of items and their average correlations. Thus, when a Cronbach Alpha value is small, the test is either too short or the items have very little in common and vice versa (Nunnally & Bernstein, 1994). This method has been recommended by (Churchill Jr., 1979, 1987; Nunnally & Bernstein, 1994) and used in numerous other studies (Crook & Booth, 1997; Gardner, 1985; Henthorne et al., 1993; A. A. Mitchell & Olson, 1981; Petersen, 1992; Walker & Dubitsky, 1994).

Other factors that could not be looked at using Alpha were determined through correlations and similar method has also been utilized by other researchers (Koslow et al., 1994; Touchstone et al., 1999) as a way to denote reliability for scales that only have two items. The higher the correlation, the greater the internal consistency and therefore the greater the reliability of the measure (Bagozzi, 1994).

Validity Evaluation
Validity is synonymous with the accuracy of the measuring instrument. It is defined as the degree to which what is observed or measured, is the same as what was purported to be observed or measured (R. Rosenthal & Rosnow, 1991). External validity relates to the degree of generalizability and internal validity, which relates to the degree of validity of statements made about whether X causes Y (R. Rosenthal & Rosnow, 1991).

The method used in this research has its own inherent external validity issues. As the advertisement and product are fictitious, its external validity is limited as it is unlikely that respondents will recommend (by Word-of-Mouth) or purchase a product (Purchase Intentions) that they have never seen before. Low involvement products may also be less likely to be recommended than high involvement products. Nevertheless, respondents' differing reactions to the advertisement would be mainly related to the language and background used in the different types of advertisements, which is the main issue being investigated.

Manipulation Checks
1. Awareness
One manipulation used was the changing of the level of accommodation of the advertisement to the targeted Iban group. It was important that the respondents were unaware of the other types of advertisements and only noted and reacted to the one they were shown. Observing respondents' reaction to the advertiser's perceived sensitivity to the ethnic group allowed the researcher to check the manipulation (refer to Table 4).

Table 4 Manipulation Check

Advertisement Type	Measure*/ Ethnic**/ Variable	Advertiser's sensitivity to:								
		Iban			Malay			Chinese		
		I	M	C	I	M	C	I	M	C
Iban	M	3.8	4.7	5.0	2.9	3.0	3.6	2.8	2.8	2.9
	SD	2.0	1.6	1.4	1.7	1.6	1.3	1.6	1.5	1.2
	N	75.0	77.0	76.0	75.0	77.0	76.0	75.0	77.0	76.0
Malay	M	3.0	3.3	3.9	3.1	4.2	4.8	2.6	2.9	3.2
	SD	1.7	1.4	1.0	1.7	1.3	1.6	1.5	1.3	1.3
	N	76.0	82.0	79.0	76.0	82.0	79.0	76.0	82.0	79.0
Chinese	M	2.6	2.7	2.8	2.3	2.2	2.9	5.0	4.8	4.9
	SD	1.6	1.4	1.3	1.4	1.2	1.3	1.7	2.1	1.2
	N	75.0	80.0	83.0	75.0	80.0	83.0	75.0	80.0	83.0
Malay and Iban	M	3.6	4.4	5.1	3.4	4.0	4.7	2.6	3.2	3.5
	SD	2.0	1.7	1.3	1.8	1.6	0.9	1.5	1.7	1.4
	N	75.0	76.0	77.0	75.0	76.0	77.0	75.0	76.0	77.0
Malay and Chinese	M	3.1	3.6	3.7	3.0	3.8	3.6	3.5	3.8	3.8
	SD	1.9	1.5	1.2	1.7	1.5	1.1	1.7	1.6	1.2
	N	75.0	90.0	77.0	75.0	90.0	77.0	75.0	90.0	77.0

* M – Mean, SD – Std. Deviation, N – Sample Size; ** I – Iban, M – Malay, C – Chinese

The two-way MANOVA main effects (ethnicity, advertisement type) were found to be significant (Pillai = 0.049, F = 2.425, p < 0. 0001) with the advertiser's sensitivity to Iban (F = 2.317, p < 0.018) and Malay (F = 4.069, p < 0.0001) significant while sensitivity to Chinese was not significant (F = 1.592, p < 0.123). This demonstrates that there is a difference in respondents' views to the advertiser's sensitivity to Malay and Iban by advertisement type and ethnicity.

A further MANOVA was carried out to determine the impact of ethnic identification strength and social distance. The three-way MANOVA main effect for ethnic identification strength was found to be significant (Pillai = 0.091, F = 2.971, p < 0. 0001). Advertiser's sensitivity to Iban (F = 2.807, p < 0.001), Malay (F = 2.910, p < 0.001) and Chinese (F = 2.284, p < 0.007) was significant. This measurement takes into account within group effects (Gao et al., 1994) and demonstrates that there is a difference in respondents' view to advertiser's sensitivity to Malay, Iban and Chinese by advertisement type, ethnicity and ethnic identification.

The three-way MANOVA main effect for social distance was found to be significant (Pillai = 0.057, F = 1.868, p < 0. 006). The advertiser's sensitivity to Iban (F = 3.233, p < 0.001) was the only significant variable. The advertiser's sensitivity to Malay (F = 1.033, p < 0.409) and Chinese (F = 1.294, p < 0.243) was not significant. This measurement takes into account between group distance (Bogardus, 1967) and demonstrates that there is a difference in respondents' views of the advertiser's sensitivity to Iban by advertisement type, ethnicity and social distance.

2. Homogeneity across advertisement types by ethnic groups
Another issue that was checked was that the ethnic groups were homogeneous and comparable across advertisement types. One manipulation used was the advertisement

type used in the questionnaires. It was important that the respondents were unaware of the other types of advertisements and only noted and reacted to the one they were shown. Therefore there may be heterogeneity in the groups by the different advertisement types, which would not allow for comparison.

It was noted that the respondents that saw the advertisements were Malays, Chinese, or Iban whether they were similar across a number of variables for each advertisement type. This provided some confirmation of homogeneity across the advertisement types for each ethnic group. This was ascertained in two ways. The first was by declaration, in which each respondent stated that they were of a specific ethnic group. The second was to test that the viewers of the different types of advertisement were similar across demographic variables and social distance, which are variables not directly connected to the tests conducted for the advertisements. This was tested by ANOVA for social distance and Chi-Sq test for the demographic variables.

For Iban, the results for all demographic variables including gender (Chi Sq = 7.367, $p < 0.118$), age (Chi Sq = 159.93, $p < 0.398$) and education (Chi Sq = 25.94, $p < 0.168$) were not significant. For Malays, only education (Chi Sq = 50.46, $p < 0.001$) was significant and all other demographic variables including gender (Chi Sq = 1.306, $p < 0.860$), age (Chi Sq = 171.31, $p < 0.190$) and social distance (F = 1.062, $p < 0.375$) were not significant. For Chinese, all demographic variables including gender (Chi Sq = 2.903, $p < 0.574$), age (Chi Sq = 161.03, $p < 0.219$), education (Chi Sq = 22.36, $p < 0.321$) and social distance (F = 0.977, $p < 0.420$) were not significant. This suggests homogeneity by ethnic group across the advertisement types.

3. Sample Size
Another important issue was that the sample size in the manipulations was acceptable. The sample sizes in cells in the manipulation tables were: in the range of 75 to 90 for the first factorial design to note the impact of ethnicity and advertisement type; in the range of 25 to 61 for the second factorial design to note the impact of ethnic identification strength; and were in the range of 21 to 56 for the third factorial design to note the impact of social distance. The first factorial design had 15 cells between subjects and the second and third had 30 cells between subjects. Other studies utilized a lesser number per cell [e.g. 15 per cell in (M. E. Goldberg & Gorn, 1974)] to higher numbers per cell [e.g. 80 per cell in (Clarke, 1984)].

5. FINDINGS

The first three propositions address the issue of interaction between ethnicity and the different advertisement types. Each main proposition was broken down into four sub-propositions, to assess the unintended effects of ethnically targeted advertising on emotions, attitudes towards the advertisement, attitudes towards the company and behavioral intentions. P_1 addresses the issue of the unintended reactions of non-target readers to a fully, or partially, accommodated advertisement that targets another ethnic group. P_2 addresses the relationships of accommodation attempts and the reactions of Malay, Iban and Chinese respondents. P_3 specifically looks at how the dominant ethnic group (Malay) and two non-dominant ethnic groups (Chinese and Iban) react to novel advertisements, in the Malaysian context (that use unexpected cues, i.e. language), as compared to a standard advertisement (that incorporates commonly used cues, i.e. language).

A summary of the proposition findings is explained for Malay, Chinese and Iban respondents in Table 10, 16 and 17.

Targeting

Overall, the findings suggest that there are relationships between ethnicity, advertisement type and ethnic identification and the variables studied. Many of the interactions are partial. Nearly all propositions show partial negative emotional reaction. However, this does not translate into other attitudinal or behavioral intentions except in specific instances, e.g. referring to Chinese language advertisements. Malay and Iban reactions are similar for nearly all the issues studied.

There is no significant difference in the non-dominant groups' reaction to their language advertisement compared to the standard advertisement, while the dominant ethnic group reacts negatively to novel advertisements. There is also a weak relationship between weak and strong ethnic identifiers.

Although Malay respondents had some limited negative emotional reactions to the Iban language advertisement, these were not accompanied by negative attitudes to the advertisement or to the company. However, for the Chinese language advertisement, there was stronger evidence of negative reactions, including emotions, attitudes to the advertisement, attitudes to the company and behavioral intentions.
Iban respondents had some limited negative emotional reactions to the Malay language advertisement. The negative emotional reactions were not accompanied by negative attitudes to the advertisement or to the company. However, for the Chinese language advertisement, there was stronger evidence of negative reactions, including emotions, attitudes to the advertisement, attitudes to the company and behavioral intentions.

Chinese respondents had some limited negative emotional reactions to the Malay and Iban language advertisements. The negative emotional reactions were not accompanied by negative attitudes to the advertisement or to the company, though (Refer to Table 5).

54

Table 5 Findings for Proposition 1

Ethnic group	Variables	Advertisement Targeted To:					
		Malay		Iban		Chinese	
		P*	F*	P	F	P	F
Malay	Emotion			(-)	(-)	(-)	(-)
	A_{AD}			(-)	NS	(-)	(-)
	A_{CO}			(-)	NS	(-)	(-)
	Behavioral Intention			(-)	NS	(-)	(-)
Iban	Emotion	(-)	(-)			(-)	(-)
	A_{AD}	(-)	NS			(-)	(-)
	A_{CO}	(-)	NS			(-)	(-)
	Behavioral Intention	(-)	NS			(-)	(-)
Chinese	Emotion	(-)	(-)	(-)	(-)		
	A_{AD}	(-)	NS	(-)	NS		
	A_{CO}	(-)	NS	(-)	NS		
	Behavioral Intention	(-)	NS	(-)	NS		

* P – Posited, F – Finding, (positive, negative, or not significant)

Accommodation

Malay respondents' negative emotional reactions to the Iban language advertisement were limited to alienation and feeling targeted. The negative emotional reactions were not accompanied by negative attitudes towards the advertisement or the company. However, in the case of Malays who viewed Chinese language advertisements, there was partial support for the posited negative emotional reactions and full support for the posited negative attitudes to the advertisement, attitudes to the company and behavioral intentions.

Iban respondents reacted similarly to Malay respondents. Negative reactions to the Malay language advertisements were limited to negative emotional responses. The negative emotional reactions were not accompanied by negative attitudes to the advertisement or to the company, though. However, in the case of Iban who viewed Chinese language advertisements, there was support for the posited negative emotional, attitude to the advertisement, attitude to the company and behavioral intentions.

Chinese respondents, on the other hand, only reacted negatively towards the Malay and Iban language advertisements in terms of their response on one emotional variable item; feeling targeted. This was not accompanied by negative attitudes to the advertisement, company, or behavioral intentions, though (Refer to Table 6).

Table 6 Findings for Proposition 2

Ethnic group	Variables	Advertisement Accommodated To:					
		Malay		Iban		Chinese	
		P*	F*	P*	F*	P*	F*
Malay	Emotion			(-)	(-)	(-)	(-)
	A_{AD}			(-)	NS	(-)	(-)
	A_{CO}			(-)	NS	(-)	(-)
	Behavioral Intention			(-)	NS	(-)	(-)
Iban	Emotion	(-)	NS			(-)	(-)
	A_{AD}	(-)	NS			(-)	(-)
	A_{CO}	(-)	NS			(-)	(-)
	Behavioral Intention	(-)	NS			(-)	(-)
Chinese	Emotion	(-)	NS	(-)	NS		
	A_{AD}	(-)	NS	(-)	NS		
	A_{CO}	(-)	NS	(-)	NS		
	Behavioral Intention	(-)	NS	(-)	NS		

* P – Posited, F – Finding, (negative, positive, not significant)

Standard and Novel Advertisements – Dominant Ethnic Group

The findings for Propositions 3 indicate that the dominant group (Malay) reacts negatively to the novel advertisement in the Chinese language. This does not occur for the Iban language advertisement except for a partial emotional response (alienation) (Refer to Table 7).

Table 7 Findings for Proposition 3 (Dominant Group)

Ethnic group	Variables	Novel Advertisement			
		Iban		Chinese	
		P*	F*	P*	F*
Malay	Emotion	(-)	(-)	(-)	(-)
	A_{AD}	(-)	NS	(-)	(-)
	A_{CO}	(-)	NS	(-)	(-)
	Behavioral Intention	(-)	NS	(-)	(-)

* P – Posited, F – Finding, (negative, positive, not significant)

Standard and Novel Advertisements – Non-Dominant Ethnic Group

The findings indicate that there are no significant differences in reactions by Chinese respondents to the Iban language advertisement as compared to the Malay language advertisement. This was also the case for the novel Chinese language advertisement, with the exception of a stronger emotional (feeling targeted) response.

As for Iban respondents, there was no significant difference in their reactions to the Iban language advertisement compared to the Malay language advertisement. For the novel Chinese language advertisement, the following reactions were significantly more negative: feeling targeted; attitude to the advertisement; affective reaction to the advertisement; attitude to the brand; corporate credibility; rapport; rapport relationship; purchase intention; and WOM (Refer to Table 8).

Table 8 Findings for Proposition 3 (Non-Dominant Groups)

Ethnic group	Variables	Novel Advertisement			
		Iban		Chinese	
		P*	F*	P*	F*
Iban	Emotion	(+)	NS	(-)	(-)
	A $_{AD}$	(+)	NS	(-)	(-)
	A $_{CO}$	(+)	NS	(-)	(-)
	Behavioral Intention	(+)	NS	(-)	(-)
Chinese	Emotion	(-)	NS	(+)	NS
	A $_{AD}$	(-)	NS	(+)	NS
	A $_{CO}$	(-)	NS	(+)	NS
	Behavioral Intention	(-)	NS	(+)	NS

* P – Posited, F – Finding, (negative, positive, not significant)

Within Group Differences

The findings indicate that overall, there were few differences in the reactions of weak and strong ethnic identifiers that were not targeted by the accommodated advertisement. The few differences that did occur were limited to a few emotional reactions (Refer to Table 9 for a depiction of the findings).

Between Group Differences

The MANOVA tests indicated no interactions between the variables. Therefore, there appears to be no relationship between social distance and the variables studied.

Table 9 Findings for Proposition 4 – Targeted Advertisement

Ethnic group	Variables	Advertisement Targeted To:					
		Malay		Iban		Chinese	
		P*	F*	P	F	P	F
Malay	Emotion			(-)	NS	(-)	(-, Overall Emotion)
	A $_{AD}$			(-)	NS	(-)	NS
	A $_{CO}$			(-)	NS	(-)	NS
	Behavioral Intention			(-)	NS	(-)	NS
Iban	Emotion	(-)	(-, Overall Emotion and Threatened)			(-)	NS
	A $_{AD}$	(-)	NS			(-)	NS
	A $_{CO}$	(-)	NS			(-)	NS
	Behavioral Intention	(-)	+			(-)	NS
Chinese	Emotion	(-)	NS	(-)	NS		
	A $_{AD}$	(-)	NS	(-)	NS		
	A $_{CO}$	(-)	NS (-, affect)	(-)	NS		
	Behavioral Intention	(-)	NS	(-)	NS		

* P – Posited, F – Finding, NS – no significant difference

Qualitative Data

Respondents were given the opportunity to state why they liked or disliked the particular advertisement that they saw. Overall, there were more negative reactions than positive, with the Chinese language advertisement scoring the highest number of negative statements. The Bahasa Malaysia language advertisement obtained the most positive statements. Please refer to Table 13 for a summary of the statements by number and Appendix 1 for the full list of statements.

Table 10 Summary of Proposition Findings for Malay Respondents

Proposition	P1 (-)		(-)	P2 (-)	(-)	P3 (-)	(-)	P4 (-)	(-)	(-)	P5
Advertisement Type / Variables	I	M	C	M, MI, I	M, MC, C	I	C	I	M	C	
Overall Emotions	X	-	X	X	X	X	X	X	-	X	M
Alienation	✓	-	X	✓	✓	✓	✓	X	-	X	M
Anger	✓	-	X	X	X	X	X	M	-	M	M
Targeted	✓	-	✓	✓	✓	✓	✓	M	-	M	M
Threatened	X	-	X	X	X	X	X	X	-	X	M
Att tow the Advertisement	X	-	✓	X	✓	X	✓	X	-	X	M
Affect tow the Advertisement	X	-	✓	X	✓	X	✓	X	-	X	M
Att tow the product	X	-	✓	X	✓	X	✓	X	-	X	M
Att tow the brand	X	-	✓	X	✓	X	✓	X	-	X	M
Att tow the Company	X	-	✓	X	✓	X	✓	M	-	M	M
Corporate Credibility	X	-	✓	X	✓	X	✓	M	-	M	M
Corporate Image	X	-	✓	X	✓	X	✓	X	-	X	M
Rapport	X	-	✓	X	✓	X	✓	X	-	X	M
Rapport R'ship	X	-	✓	X	✓	X	✓	X	-	X	M
Rapport Trust	X	-	✓	X	✓	X	✓	X	-	X	M
Purchase Intention	X	-	✓	X	✓	X	✓	M	-	M	M
WOM	X	-	X	X	✓	X	✓	X	-	X	M

* X - proposition rejected; - Not Applicable; ✓ proposition accepted; M – Not significant at MANOVA and GLM; I – Iban, M – Malay, C – Chinese, MI – Malay and Iban, MC – Malay and Chinese; P – partial acceptance

Table 11 Summary of Proposition Findings for Chinese Respondents

Proposition	P1			P2		P3		P4			P5
	(-)	(-)		(-)	(-)	(-)	(+)	(-)	(-)	(-)	
Advertisement Type / Variables	I	M	C	C, MC, I	C, MC, M	I	C	I	M	C	
Overall Emotions	X	X	-	X	X	X	X	X	X	-	M
Alienation	X	✓	-	X	X	X	X	X	X	-	M
Anger	✓	✓	-	X	X	X	X	M	M	-	M
Targeted	✓	X	-	✓	✓	X	✓	M	M	-	M
Threatened	X	X	-	X	X	X	X	X	X	-	M
Att tow the Advertisement	X	X	-	X	X	X	X	X	X	-	M
Affect tow the Advertisement	X	X	-	X	X	X	X	X	✓	-	M
Att tow the product	X	X	-	X	X	X	X	X	X	-	M
Att tow the brand	X	X	-	X	X	X	X	X	X	-	M
Att tow the Company	X	X	-	X	X	X	X	M	M	-	M
Corporate Credibility	X	X	-	X	X	X	X	M	M	-	M
Corporate Image	X	X	-	X	X	X	X	X	X	-	M
Rapport	X	X	-	X	X	X	X	X	X	-	M
Rapport R'ship	X	X	-	X	X	X	X	X	X	-	M
Rapport Trust	X	X	-	X	X	X	X	X	X	-	M
Purchase Intention	X	X	-	X	X	X	X	M	M	-	M
WOM	X	X	-	X	X	X	X	X	X	-	M

* X - proposition rejected; - Not Applicable; ✓ proposition accepted; M – Not significant at MANOVA and GLM; I – Iban, M – Malay, C – Chinese, MI – Malay and Iban, MC – Malay and Chinese; P – partial acceptance

Table 12 Summary of Proposition Findings for Iban Respondents

Proposition	P1			P2		P3		P4			P5
	(-)	(-)	(-)	(-)	(-)	(+)	(-)	(-)	(-)	
Advertisement Type / Variables	I	M	C	I, MI, M	I, MC, C	C	I	I	M	C	
Overall Emotions	-	X	X	X	X	X	X	-	✓	X	M
Alienation	-	X	X	X	X	X	X	-	X	X	M
Anger	-	X	X	X	X	X	X	-	M	M	M
Targeted	-	X	✓	X	✓	✓	X	-	M	M	M
Threatened	-	✓	X	X	X	X	X	-	✓	X	M
Att tow the Advertisement	-	X	✓	X	✓	✓	X	-	X	X	M
Affect tow the Advertisement	-	X	X	X	X	✓	X	-	X	X	M
Att tow the product	-	X	✓	X	X	X	X	-	X	X	M
Att tow the brand	-	X	✓	X	✓	✓	X	-	X	X	M
Att tow the Company	-	X	X	X	✓	X	X	-	M	M	M
Corporate Credibility	-	X	✓	X	✓	✓	X	-	M	M	M
Corporate Image	-	X	X	X	✓	X	X	-	X	X	M
Rapport	-	X	✓	X	✓	✓	X	-	X	X	M
Rapport R'ship	-	X	✓	X	✓	✓	X	-	X	X	M
Rapport Trust	-	X	✓	X	X	X	X	-	X	X	M
Purchase Intention	-	X	✓	X	✓	✓	X	-	M	M	M
WOM	-	X	X	X	✓	✓	X	-	X	X	M

* X - proposition rejected; - Not Applicable; ✓ proposition accepted; M – Not significant at MANOVA and GLM; I – Iban, M – Malay, C – Chinese, MI – Malay and Iban, MC – Malay and Chinese; P – partial acceptance

Table 13 Number Of Statements to Different Advertisements by Ethnic Group

Reaction by ethnic group / Advertisement Type	Like					Dislike				
	Iban	Malay	Chi-nese	Total		Iban	Malay	Chi-nese	Total	
				No	%				No.	%
Advertisement 1 – Iban	7	0	0	7	19	7	11	4	23	21
Advertisement 2 – Malay	3	7	1	11	31	4	5	2	11	10
Advertisement 3 – Chinese	4	1	1	6	17	12	19	4	36	34
Advertisement 4 – Malay and Iban	2	4	0	6	17	5	13	6	24	22
Advertisement 5 – Malay and Chinese	2	2	2	6	17	4	5	4	13	12
Total	18	14	4	36	100	32	53	20	107	100

These comments were sorted into eight groups based on language, the advertisement design, racial statements, targeted, 'Halal[1]', Malay language, ethnicity and English language and are summarized in Table 14. Please refer to Appendix 1 for the full list of statements.

Most advertisements generated comments that were based on the language used in the advertisement such as "Like because used Iban language (E256, M, 35, De, I, 4)[2]" or "Don't like the use of Chinese (E310, M, 25, S, I, 4)".

A few commented on the advertisement design "Don't like because used the Iban language and uses a traditional and conservative layout (E15, M, 22, S, M, 6, 4)", "Beautiful, attract attention, language easy to understand and price shown clearly (E91, F, 20, S, M, 6, 1)", and "Don't like because of the color. Not interesting (E100, M, 21, S, C, 5,2)."

Other comments were based on racial statements such as "Don't like because this advertisement is racist. Looks like it emphasizes only Iban, even though the background is more Malay. I am not confident of this advertisement (D016, F, 20, S, M, 6, 4)" or "Don't give full information about the product (Halal or not). Can create sensitive racial issues. This is Malaysia not China (D065, F, 25, S, M, 6, 2)."

The comments also show that respondents were aware that the advertisements were being targeted to other groups, e.g. "The brand is aimed at a specific ethnic group, as a Muslim, I am cautious of its contents (E715, F, 42, S, M, 3, 1)." This statement comes across with a 'halal' message, as do a number of other statements such as "Don't have 'halal' sign (E72, M, 23, Di, M, 6, 1)" or "No 'halal' logo for Muslims (E91, F, 20, S, M, 6, 2)."

---

[1] Halal is an Arabic term meaning, "permitted, allowed lawful or licit." When used in relationship to food or drink, means "permissible" for consumption by a Muslim.

[2] Details beside comments, i.e. (E15, M, 22, S, M, 6, 4) is arranged as follows: Identity No., Sex (M, F), Age, Education (N – No formal education, S- Secondary School, Di – Diploma, De – Degree, M – Masters, P - PhD), Ethnicity (I – Iban, M - Malay, C – Chinese), Ethnic Identity Strength (1 to 7, where 7 is the strongest), Social Distance to Iban (1 – 7, where 7 is the furthest social distance).

Table 14 Breakdown of Number of Statements by Reaction and Ethnic Group

Reaction / Ethnic Group / Advertisement Type		Advertisement 1 – Iban	Advertisement 2 – Malay	Advertisement 3 – Chinese	Advertisement 4 – Malay and Iban	Advertisement 5 – Malay and Chinese
Language	Iban	8	1	8	1	2
	Malay	6	1	13	3	1
	Chinese	3	1	3	5	2
Advertisement Design	Iban	2	4	3	3	3
	Malay	2	6	2	4	0
	Chinese	0	1	1	0	4
Racial	Iban	1	2	3	2	3
	Malay	1	0	4	5	1
	Chinese	1	2	2	3	0
Targeted	Iban	5	2	5	2	1
	Malay	2	0	3	3	1
	Chinese	0	1	0	0	0
Halal	Iban	1	0	1	0	0
	Malay	2	2	3	7	3
	Chinese	0	0	0	0	0
Malay	Iban	1	0	0	3	0
	Malay	4	4	4	4	0
	Chinese	0	0	0	0	0
Ethnic	Iban	0	5	6	1	1
	Malay	0	3	1	3	1
	Chinese	0	1	1	1	1
English	Iban	0	0	0	0	0
	Malay	0	0	0	0	1
	Chinese	0	0	0	0	1

This feeling is also translated into the need for the use of the national language, Bahasa Malaysia, in statements such as "Use Bahasa Malaysia (E302, F, 33, S, M, 3, 2)" and ethnic based comments such as "Don't like because too simple and uses only Iban ethnic elements. It should use all elements of all ethnicities to make it more pleasing (E25, F, 22, Di, M, 5, 1)."

Request for an English language based advertisement only appeared for the composite advertisement of Iban background and Malay and Chinese language. The only two statements on the use of English were "No English statement about the drink (E1026, M, 43, S, C, 4, 1)" and "Don't like because does not use an international *lingua franca*, i.e. English. Easier and able to be understood by all (D009, F, 20, S, M, 6, 2)."

6. WHAT DOES IT ALL MEAN?

Contextual Influences

The context and method chosen to test the model and propositions may have a bearing on the findings. This research uses ethnically targeted advertising in a Malaysian context. Effects from the different ethnic groups' social hierarchies and Malaysian social situation may have an impact on the findings. It is therefore important to understand the situation in Malaysia in order to interpret and evaluate the findings.

In Malaysia, advertisements using various languages and language mixes are extensively shown on television, depicted in print, or spoken over the radio. Therefore, there is a level of awareness and an acceptance of different languages used in advertising. It would not be a surprise to a Malaysian to see an all-Chinese language advertisement on television or print. Therefore the possibility of someone from a particular ethnic group seeing a different language advertisement is quite high.

Malaysia is a plural society (Furnivall, 1948) and not a melting pot of ethnic groups. Due to this separateness, there has been a push from the government to integrate ethnic groups into the dominant group (Anonymous, 2002; Joseph & Holden, 2001). As stated by Dr. Mahathir Mohamad, Malaysia's previous Prime Minister, "What we want to do is to integrate different races and different tribal groups into one society, each one playing its own role with no one higher than the other...this (integration) has worked very well but not assimilation" (Anonymous, 2002): 1). This is achieved by education and integration activities (Watson, 1980b). The integration activities are based on the concept that uncoupling the bonds of nationality and culture will lead to open and equal communication (Dijkstra, Geuijen, & de Ruijter, 2001). It must be understood that common language, symbols, rituals and stories are not sufficient to ensure societal integration, unless there is some level of cultural identity (Anonymous, 2000; Schudson, 1994).

The fully targeted group in this research was Iban. This choice was based on theory (e.g. small by numbers and a distinct group) (Deshpande & Stayman, 1994; McGuire, 1984; McGuire & McGuire, 1979, 1981; Pollak & Niemann, 1998). However, the findings indicate a closer social link between Iban and Malay respondents (S. A. Grier & Deshpande, 2001; Moscovisi, 1975; Oakes, 1987; Tajfel, 1981) than was expected. Iban respondents appear to be integrated into the dominant culture based on their responses to questions about their reaction to the advertisements, language and lifestyle (Noriah, 1994; Postill, 1999; Tawai, 1997). This supports the idea that the social context should to be taken into account when considering the distinctiveness of ethnic groups.

Questions about "perceived threat" provided a clearer picture of the closeness of Iban to Malay. Iban felt more threatened when viewing their own Iban language advertisement as compared to Malay or Chinese language advertisements. This fear of standing out against the dominant culture suggests a cultural persona that does not wish to be distanced from the dominant group, or to be distinct. It clearly shows that Iban are threatened by advertisements that target them and this suggests that they are acculturated to the dominant group, have accepted the integration efforts of the government, and / or, are socially afraid to stand out against the dominant group. Malay respondents on the other hand did not feel threatened by the Iban language advertisement as Malay respondents belong to the dominant group and appear to be close enough culturally to Iban to understand that such an advertisement is not targeting them.

This reaction by Iban respondents may have been influenced by individual attitudes and values. Individuals have considerable autonomy over which behaviors to adopt from the dominant culture and which behaviors to retain from their original culture (Burton, 1996). A construct, such as language, is a private activity that is determined primarily by one's own choice (W. Lee & Tse, 1994b), although there may be structural constraints that force compliance (Wallendorf & Reilly, 1983). In Malaysia's advertising industry these constraints are codified (ACTR, 1990; Adnan, 1994; Faiza, 2001; Joseph & Holden, 2001) and have to be followed. Therefore, the use of the targeted group's language in the advertisement should be attractive to Iban respondents and should encourage Iban to score higher on all dimensions than other groups. This did not occur, possibly due to the individuals' choice to not deviate from the dominant ethnic worldview (Whorf, 1941) and to comply with the perceived Malaysian government agenda for integration (Joseph & Holden, 2001).

When the question of a product is brought into the equation, there could be varying degrees of acculturation that may have affected the respondents' reaction to the advertisements. Some consumption behaviors may be ingrained in an ethnic identity and therefore less likely to change regardless of the extent of time and interaction with the dominant culture. Other, less culturally important, behaviors could change easily (W. Lee & Tse, 1994a). The use of an ethnically neutral product may have inhibited the reactions to the advertisement and reactions to the company by Iban respondents, but clearly did not inhibit Malay respondents, as they questioned whether the drink was 'halal' or not, referring to their sociotype and/or stereotype of Iban people as drunkards. This can be seen from comments by respondents about the targeted advertisements; "The brand is aimed at a specific ethnic group, as a Muslim, I am cautious of its contents (E715, F, 42, S, M, 3, 1)" and "Don't like because the drink in the advertisement is unknown, what type is it and Iban language is extremely difficult to understand (E701, F, 49, N, M, 7, 2)." Even an Iban questioned the drink in the advertisement: "Advertisement like this shows that this product is specifically for Iban and that the probability that this drink is alcoholic is high (E896, F, 20, S, I, 3)."

Apparently Iban knew they were targeted, did not like the idea of an 'alcoholic' drink (their own perception and stereotype) and assumed that the company targeting them was doing so because they were 'easy' target and that the advertisement was not ethnically inclusive and a non-integration advertisement. These perceptions are depicted by the following comments by Iban respondents: "Advertisement like this shows that this product is specifically for Iban and that the probability that this drink is alcoholic is high (E896, F, 20, S, I, 3);" "Don't like because this advertisement too weighted towards the capture of Iban customers hearts (E255, M, 32, D, I, 5);" "Too aimed to Iban only and not including other races (E252, F, 36, S, I, 5);" "The language used in the advertisement is aimed to a certain ethnic group that the company thinks is easier to deceive (E461, M, 40, S, I, 6);" "Don't like the mixture of language like using 'sensasi', try to use more suitable Iban word (E259, M, 39, Di, I, 4);" "Don't like because leaning too much to one type only, that is focusing on Iban only. Bahasa Melayu should be used to make it easier for customers of all types of races (E254, F, 34, S, I, 4)."

This suggests that Iban are not as socially distinct and different to Malay respondents as previously expected. Iban reactions tended to mimic those of Malay respondents, reactions even though they still identified strongly with Iban. Other studies have found that it is not uncommon for someone in a minority group to speak and act as if they were in the main ethnic group but remain strongly psychologically attached to his or her group of origin (Penaloza, 1994).

Chinese respondents, on the other hand, have a clearly different language and culture to Malay (Andaya & Andaya, 1982; K. H. Lee & Tan, 2000; J. Platt, 1981). This may be due to the numerical status of Chinese as it is large enough to withstand the push from the government for integration. In 1999, there was an estimated 5,597,900 Chinese in Malaysia (Jabatan Perangkaan Malaysia, 1999; Mardiana, 2000). This makes them distinct and therefore likely to react differently, to the targeted advertisements than Malay or Iban respondents.

Chinese reactions may be influenced by the situation in Malaysia where there is a form of 'tall poppy' syndrome. This is where no one wants to stand out by criticizing another ethnic group, thus creating disharmony. This is in line with the cultural schema of a non-dominant ethnic group, where the group is aware of its own cultural schema, as well as that of the dominant schema (Brumbaugh, 2002). This awareness allows the non-dominant group to act within social norms and expectations. It is also possible that another driving force here is the unity movement created by the government to create integration between the races (Anonymous, 2000).

Chinese respondents seem to prefer the partially accommodated Chinese language advertisements. This preference appears to support comments by Malaysia's previous Prime Minister Dr. Mahathir Mohamad that:

"... The vast majority of Chinese are very tolerant. They understand the reasons behind the policy of positive discrimination. They have seen what has happened in other countries where there is no attempt to equalize the development of the different communities and how people take it out on Chinese community... (Anonymous, 2001a): 1)."

Previous studies have also noted that social reference may be founded upon historical group circumstances and group membership (Servaes, 1989; E. J. Smith, 1989, 1991). The greatest historical issue for Malay and Chinese was the May 13 1969 incident[3] where Chinese suffered greatly (Anonymous, 2000). The Chinese are also aware of their group membership and the social power held by Malays and therefore react accordingly (Depret & Fiske, 1993; Deschamps, 1982). This can be seen by their preference for a partially accommodated advertisement (i.e. an advertisement that has both the dominant language and their own language in it).

Malay and Chinese language advertisements with an Iban background elicited a number of positive comments from all three ethnic groups. These included: "Like it

---

[3] The 13 May 1969 incident refers to ethnic riots that occurred in Malaysia.

because it attempts to involve at least one element (i.e. language) of every ethnic group (E911, F, 23, D, C, 5, 2);" "Like because it mixes 3 races in one advertisement and easy to understand (D073, M, 23, Di, M, 5, 1);" "Like because the advertisement shows that we can mix and be friends with others. Shows that Malay, Chinese and Iban can work together towards unity and cooperation (E357, F, 42, S, M, 4, 2);" "Like because easier to understand and does not neglect other races (E52, F, 20, S, I, 5)."

These comments suggest that this type of partially accommodated advertisement was seen as an ideal integration attempt and therefore there was a strong positive reaction to it by Chinese. They were angrier when viewing their own language-based advertisement than when viewing the partially accommodated advertisement as depicted in the following comments: "Don't like because background of the advertisement is not suitable and doesn't attract the attention of the consumer (E24, M, 20, S, C, 7, 5);" "Less suitable for Malaysian society because only written in Chinese (E111, F, 23, S, C, 5, 1);" and "Don't like because less honest (E109, F, 22, S, C, 6, 2)." This suggests that the integration concept promoted by the Malaysian government is working.

In the constitution of Malaysia, Malays are defined as people who speak the Malay language as their mother tongue, lead a Malay way of life and profess the Islamic faith (O. Asmah, 1983). The Malay ethnic group is the dominant ethnic group in Malaysia, both by numbers, as well as socially and culturally (O. Asmah, 1983; Jabatan Perangkaan Malaysia, 1999). Their reaction to the different advertisements was consistent with their cultural schema as the dominant group (Brumbaugh, 2002).

The dominance of Malay and their acceptance of the Malay language advertisement are clearly depicted in the following statements: "Like because it's in Bahasa Melayu (D004, F, 20, S, M, 5, 5);" "Like because uses Bahasa Melayu (E65, F, 21, S, M, 5, 1);" "Like because uses mother tongue (E53, F, 21, S, M, 5, 1);" "Like because uses Bahasa Melayu and Iban background (E38, F, 22, S, M, 7, 4)." The view that this is the most acceptable advertisement for all is depicted in the following statement: "I like this advertisement because this advertisement is not forcing and has give and take elements between all ethnicities (E321, M, 29, S, M, 5, 1)."

From a Malay viewpoint, the Chinese language advertisement is clearly unwelcome and received more negative reactions than any other advertisement (33%) (See Appendix 1 for detailed findings). The statements by Malay about the Chinese language advertisement demonstrate this sentiment. The comments include: "Don't like because don't understand the language (E87, M, 20, S, M, 6, 1);" "This advertisement places too much priority on Chinese people. I don't understand at all the language used in the advertisement (E141, M, 20, S, I, 5);" "What is the content of the tin? Suspicious of its health effects. Not written in Bahasa Melayu. Don't understand when it is nearly 70% written in Chinese (E144, M, 37, S, M, 7, 2);" "Don't like because I don't understand and furthermore it doesn't give correct details (E148, F, 48, S, M, 4, 1);" "Don't like because this advertisement stands out with one language only. Not everyone understands Chinese (E149, M, 28, S, M, 6, 5);" "This advertisement is aimed only at Iban and Chinese consumers, whereas in this country, Malay consist of a large portion of consumers (E592, M, 37, S, M, 7, 1);" and "Don't like because I don't know what this advertisement is about because the use of language that the advertisement uses and the drink is liquor and I don't like it (E425, M, 25, S, M, 6, 2)."

The Iban language advertisement was also viewed negatively by Malay respondents but less so than the Chinese language advertisement (See Appendix 1 for detailed findings). Although the comments by Malay respondents still appear harsh, there was some support for the background, which was perceived as Malay: "Don't like because written in Iban, there will be those that won't understand it (E32, F, 22, Di, M, 6, 2);" "Don't like because this advertisement is racist. Looks like it emphasizes only Iban, even though the background is more Malay. I am not confident of this advertisement (D016, F, 20, S, M, 6, 4)." The negative reactions refer more to the alcohol-based stereotype of Iban and the issue of halal and as expected suggest the need to use the dominant language: "Don't like because the drink in the advertisement is unknown, what type is it and Iban language is extremely difficult to understand (E701, F, 49, N, M, 7, 2);" "The brand is aimed at a specific ethnic group, as a Muslim, I am cautious of its contents (E715, F, 42, S, M, 3, 1);" "If possible, use Bahasa Malaysia and label as made in Sarawak (E301, M, 37, S, M, 3, 2);" "Use Bahasa Malaysia (E302, F, 33, S, M, 3, 2);" and "Did not use the official language and difficult to be understood because it is in Iban (E457, F, 24, S, M, 6, 5)".

Theoretical Discussion for Targeting

This research aims to determine the reactions of those not targeted to a targeted advertisement. This is investigated through four variables, namely emotions, attitude to the advertisement, attitude to the company and behavioral intention. It was posited that those not targeted would react more negatively to the advertisements as compared to the targeted group. However, the reactions of three ethnic groups, Malay, Iban and Chinese, offer only partial support for Proposition 1 (Refer to Table 5).

An issue raised by the findings is the distinctiveness of the subjects. It has been argued that the distinctiveness of a group is salient, when a group is a minority in numbers (Deshpande & Stayman, 1994; Pollak & Niemann, 1998). Other researchers have argued that distinctiveness is salient because of the social context (S. A. Grier & Deshpande, 2001; Moscovisi, 1975; Oakes, 1987; Tajfel, 1981). Distinctiveness theory states that the smaller the ethnic group is to the overall population, the more likely that ethnically targeted stimuli will be effective (Deshpande & Stayman, 1994). Therefore by using ethnic cues (language and background) in the advertisement, it should make distinct the differences in ethnicity of the targeted group and the non-targeted group. However, the findings indicate that this does not always occur. It appears that the Malaysian social context, (as discussed in Section 8.2), may also be influencing respondents' reactions. For a marketer, this means that targeting a group because it is a minority is insufficient. A minority group may act in a similar way to the dominant group (Penaloza, 1994). The dominant group may be accepting of the non-dominant group, but still act differently to it.

This raises the issue of ethnic dominance. It has been shown that a dominant ethnic group has only one set of cultural schema on which members may base their judgments of all other groups (Aaker et al., 2000; Brumbaugh, 2002; S. A. Grier & Brumbaugh, 1999). Interestingly, the findings suggest that the dominant group (Malay) either has an empathic perception of Iban, or that Malay respondents have more than one cultural schema, as they reacted differently to the Iban advertisement than the Chinese language advertisement. The cultural context suggests that some Malay may hold a negative view of Iban (stereotyped as drunkards), yet the reactions of Malay to the Iban language advertisement are muted. This suggests that there may be more than one node in the dominant cultural schema and/or that deviant group members assess minority groups according to their perceived similarity to the dominant group. For marketers, this suggests that a promotional program aimed at an ethnic group must take into account its status on the ethnic dominance scale.

Non-dominant ethnic groups have the dominant ethnic group's cultural schema and their own schema (Aaker et al., 2000; Brumbaugh, 2002; S. A. Grier & Brumbaugh, 1999) to create meaning of the world. The findings indicate that the non-dominant groups reacted in a similar way to the Malay language advertisement as the Malay respondents, which is understandable, as they would also have the Malay cultural schema. However, they would not have the other non-dominant ethnic group's cultural schema and should react according to the stereotype or sociotype that they hold of the other group (Katz & Braly, 1933; Triandis, 1994). This may explain why Iban reacted negatively to the Chinese language advertisement. However, the Chinese respondents appeared to be largely indifferent to the Iban language advertisement. This raises questions about non-dominant ethnic groups' cultural schema theory. Although marketers should take notice of the stereotype, or sociotype, that other groups hold about the targeted group, this must be weighed against the group's relative ethnic dominance.

The results support findings from previous studies that targeted advertisements can generate negative emotions among those not targeted (Koslow et al., 1994; Touchstone et al., 1999). Koslow et al. (1994) detailed the reactions of a non-dominant group to an advertisement in its own language and an advertisement in the dominant group's language. His findings are similar to the reactions of the Iban and Chinese readers' to Malay language advertisements. In both studies the findings indicate mainly emotional reactions. The research by Koslow et al. (1994) and Touchstone et al., (1999) is extended in this research to include the reactions of non-dominant ethnic groups (Iban and Chinese) and the dominant group (Malay) to other non-dominant groups. This study detected some negative attitudinal and behavioral reactions, particularly by Malay and Iban respondents, to Chinese language advertisements. This supports previous studies that indicate that emotional responses generated in the viewing of an advertisement can affect attitude towards the advertisement, attitude towards the brand and even purchase decisions (Batra & Ray, 1986; Holbrook & Batra, 1987). This suggests that when utilizing targeted advertising, a company may inadvertently generate negative attitudes towards the advertisement, brand and company and reduce the purchase intentions of those not targeted. Negative word of mouth could also be generated.

This ties in with the issue of how consumers behave. The findings support the CAB paradigm (e.g. cognition determines affect which determines behavior) (Holbrook, 1986); (Holbrook & Batra, 1987), particularly the role of normative belief as detailed in the theory of reasoned action (Fishbein & Ajzen, 1975; Ryan & Bonfield, 1975) and depicted in Figure 6.

Figure 6 CAB Paradigm with Normative Beliefs

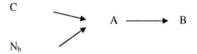

Note: C = Cognition, N_b = Normative belief, A = Affect, B = Behavior.

Consumer behavior literature suggests that emotional reaction is an important aspect of behavior. In the case of this research, the cognitive component is the processing of the advertisement. The normative belief relates to the contextual issues of ethnicity and the Malaysian context for each ethnic group, including beliefs of the expectations of important referent others and motivation to comply with those referents. This, in theory, determines affective responses and then behavior, which can be seen by the reactions of Malay and Iban respondents to the Chinese language advertisement. However, reactions to other targeted advertisements were limited to affective responses, which indicate boundaries of the paradigm. Potential explanations as to these restrictions may include distinctiveness salience and dominance issues, as discussed earlier.

Another major issue raised by the findings is the limitations of targeting. Targeting indicates a conscious choice to limit a business's products, services, promotions and activities to a specific group, while neglecting others (Kotler & Armstrong, 1994). However, this conscious choice of targeting presupposes that a particular group is important (Barnard & Ehrenberg, 1997) and neglects the effects from other groups' reactions. Another problem with the focus on one group is that the audience that views any targeted promotions is likely to include those that are not targeted (Barnard & Ehrenberg, 1997; R. W. Pollay, 1986; Steward, 1994). The focus on one group also creates problems when the company expands to use a national marketing campaign and nationwide retail chains (K. M. Freeman, 1992). The findings support the need for a broader view of targeting that accounts for possible negative emotional reactions by those not targeted. At the worst, the company may lose its credibility, image, rapport and sales. This suggests that by focusing on one group without noting the potential impact from those not targeted, is imprudent.

It is argued that a targeted communications' strategy is the most effective method of communicating with a specific ethnic group (Hecht et al., 1993; Kinra, 1997; Kumar, 2002). However, in a plural society such as Malaysia, targeted communications may cause unintended problems. The findings indicate that Iban respondents were more threatened by the Iban language advertisement than the other ethnic groups were. The advertisement may have been in their language, but socially it was perceived to be a threat. This also raises questions about the effectiveness of culturally targeted advertisement campaigns in general.

A related, and hotly debated issue in international advertising, is the efficacy of adaptation versus standardization. Adaptation can occur for the creative selling proposition, elements in the advertisement and/or the language used (Harris, 1994). The efficacy of adapted advertisements has been argued by many (R. T. Green,

Cunningham, & Cunningham, 1978; Lenormand, 1964; Shoham, 1996), but the issue raised here is the impact of the language chosen for the advertisements that are adapted to the local country and target market. As the findings indicate, if the language used in an ethnically targeted advertisement is not the dominant group's language, there is a possibility of negative reactions from those not targeted. International or cross-cultural advertising campaigns in each country should be assessed carefully in terms of cultural and social factors before proceeding. It is worth noting though, that these findings do not necessarily support the adoption of an alternative standardization strategy. This is because standardization still creates an unintended effect from those not targeted.

Segmentation based on ethnicity is not necessarily the best option even though many normative articles and books advocate it (Buck, 1998; Gazdik, 1998; Paul Herbig & Yelkur, 1998; J. D. Hill, 1999; Livingston, 1992; Nelson Jr. & Lukas, 1990; Petersen, 1992; Porter, 2002; Santoro, 1991; Segal & Sosa, 1983; Solomon, 1999; Torres & Gelb, 2002; Zbar, 1999). To be effective, segmentation requires homogeneneity within groups and heterogeneity between groups (Hoek et al., 1996; W. R. Smith, 1956). However, research indicates that there are problems with defining mutually exclusive groups and problems in measuring response elasticity (Claycamp & Massy, 1968). The findings of this research, when viewed from the cultural context, suggest that Iban readers are not as distinctly different from Malay readers as previously expected. This indicates that there are theoretical and practical weaknesses in the advocacy of an ethnic based segmentation. This is in line with Ehrenberg's work on bankcard segmentation that suggests that there are often no differences in user profiles (Kennedy & Ehrenberg, 2001).

The assumptions behind various bases used for segmentation must be questioned. The targeted Iban group appears to be a distinctive, homogeneous group, which is quite different to the other ethnic groups tested, based on responses to the validated ethnicity scale used in this study. However, the response elasticity indicates that the Iban reactions to ethnically targeted advertising are similar to those of the Malay respondents. The cultural context, as discussed earlier, also indicates similarities between Iban and Malay. This suggests that segmentation and targeting, based on ethnic grouping, may be flawed. This may be because of the confounding variables (discussed in Chapter Two and Chapter Three) such as ethnic self-awareness, cultural schema, language, meaning creation / worldview, ethnic dominance, ethnicity salience and bilingualism have been shown to impact on ethnic groups' reactions to advertisements.

The second assumption in segmenting, is that payoffs will be greater when a company matches its marketing mix to a particular segment (P. E. Green & Krieger, 1991; M. Wright, 1996). Others suggest that there is no significant difference between a segmented approach and a 'shot gun' approach (M. Wright, 1996). Recent research into how those not targeted react to targeted promotional pricing also indicate that there are negative reactions and significant costs to a company (Feinberg et al., 2002). The findings suggest that there are unintended reactions from those not targeted that may affect the profitability of current target marketing practices.

Theoretical Discussion for Accommodation

This research aims to determine the reactions of non-targeted readers who see ethnically targeted advertisements. This is further investigated by noting the reactions to advertisements that are perceived as accommodating, partially accommodating and not accommodating to them. The findings for this group of propositions provide partial support for the posited negative reaction by those who have not been accommodated.

As with the results of Proposition 1, the results for Proposition 2 again indicate that the distinctiveness of subjects is an issue. The findings also suggest support for the social context view. The contextual discussion earlier suggests that Iban are socially close to Malay and react similarly to Malay and vice versa.

As with Proposition 1, dominance is another issue raised by the findings for Proposition 2. The findings suggest that the dominant group seems to have more knowledge and acceptance of Iban, indicating stronger link to Iban than Chinese respondents. Iban respondents also reacted in a similar way to Malay respondents.

Nevertheless, a more interesting issue concerns accommodation theory. SAT plainly states that "the greater the amount of effort in accommodation that a bilingual speaker of one group was perceived to put into his message, the more favorable he would be perceived by listeners from another ethnic group and also the more effort they in turn would put into accommodating back" (H. Giles et al., 1973): 177). Accommodation theory suggests a linear relationship for the reaction to advertisements that are totally accommodated, partially accommodated and not accommodated (H. Giles et al., 1973; Simard et al., 1976). In other words, when there is a level of accommodation effort placed in an advertisement, there will be a similar level of accommodated reaction to it, creating a positive or negative linear profile for reactions to different levels of accommodation attempts.

However, the findings contradict this linear relationship level of accommodation and reactions of respondents. Instead, there was no significant difference in reactions to the advertisements that incorporated high or low levels of accommodation (refer to Table 6). This suggests that there are limits to the SAT and that, in certain instances, there will be no reaction to an accommodation attempt. The findings suggest that this occurs when the accommodated group is seen as similar, dominant, or unknown to a non-dominant group. From a promotional strategy viewpoint, this indicates that there will be instances where it is not worthwhile adapting advertisements to suite ethnic requirements.

On the other hand, the findings suggest that for non-dominant respondents, there is a curvilinear profile in their reaction to different levels of accommodation (refer to Table 15). Instead of a negative or a non-significant reaction, there is a stronger or weaker reaction (for some variables), for the 'middle ground' advertisements viewed by Chinese and Iban respondents. This creates a curvilinear reaction profile, as opposed to the expected linear reaction profile.

Table 15 Instances of Curvilinear Reaction

Variable / Ethnicity / Advertisement type	Iban respondents			Chinese respondents		
	Malay language	Malay and Iban language	Iban language	Chinese language	Malay and Chinese language	Iban language
Affect towards the Advertisement*	3.4	4.2	2.7	-	-	-
Attitude towards the Product*	3.3	3.9	3.1	-	-	-
Overall emotions**	-	-	-	4	3.3	3.7
Anger**	-	-	-	3.6	3.1	3.9

* Higher number indicates a more positive reaction, ** Higher number indicates a more negative reaction

A previous study also found a curvilinear relationship between adaptation and attraction (Francis, 1991). The study by (Francis, 1991) investigated the social adaptation process, which is similar to accommodation. The study utilized three levels of cultural adaptation to investigate Americans' responses to the selling behavior of a Japanese sales team. The results showed that the 'middle ground' selling behavior was most attractive (i.e. the Japanese sales team's members retained some of their stereotypical style but showed speech adaptation through the use of less formal speech with minor attempts at token American conventions such as hand shakes, less formal dress, more individuality and directness in the communication process (Francis, 1991): 412). However, other studies that replicated this experiment in an Asian context did not find a curvilinear reaction (Pornpitakpan, 1999);(Pornpitakpan, 2003). Rather, there was a linear reaction.

SAT has been developed on the basis of linguistics and emotional reaction (H. Giles et al., 1973) and has neglected to note other factors such as social and cultural issues that may impact on the reaction to accommodation. It is suggested by the findings that accommodation theory is limited to the cultural schema and perceived closeness of the group being targeted to other non-targeted groups. Another caveat may be that if external pressures (Simard et al., 1976) are too strong, then it impinges upon the decision making of ethnic groups to the extent that they would prefer a partially accommodated advertisement to their own fully accommodated advertisement. Therefore, the findings suggest that there are bounds to accommodation theory, especially when it is placed in an ethnic advertising context.

Another issue arising from the findings relates to the international advertising literature perspective. International advertising is concerned with standardization, contingency perspective, or adaptation arguments (Agrawal, 1995). This is analogous to the non-accommodated, partially accommodated and fully accommodated advertisements as utilized in this research. However, instead of looking at the reactions of those targeted, the research looks at the reactions of those who are not targeted. This provides a whole new area to be explored in international advertising. The implications are that there could be unexpected consequences (or unintended effects) of using standardization, contingency perspective, or adaptation strategies in the international marketing context.

The findings suggest that there are two likely reactions by non-targeted groups to advertisements that incorporate high levels of accommodation, either indifferent or negative responses. The reactions may be influenced of ethnic dominance, distinctiveness of the ethnic group and/or the social context in Malaysia. Many international advertising studies depict strong preference for adapted advertisements by those who are targeted (Shoham, 1996; Ueltschy & Ryans Jr., 1997). However, the question of non-targeted groups' reactions has been ignored.

The findings that the 'middle ground' advertisements resulted in positive curvilinear effect for specific variables may have implications for the contingency view of international advertising. There are scholars who advocate a combination of both perspectives (standardization and adaptation), depending upon the country it is used in (Kotler, 1986; Walters, 1986). The findings here suggest that there are merits for such a view. The curvilinear reaction to accommodation depicts a positive emotional and attitudinal reaction to 'middle ground' advertisements. However, this only occurs for non-dominant groups. Promotional campaigns in each country should therefore be assessed carefully in terms of opportunity costs and trade offs from targeting specific markets. A close consideration of cultural and social factors appears to be critical.

Theoretical Discussion for Standard and Novel Advertisements – Dominant Ethnic Group

This research aims to determine the reactions of those not targeted (in this instance, the dominant ethnic group) to targeted advertisements. This is further investigated by noting the reactions of readers to advertisements that are perceived as novel advertisements compared to a standard advertisement.

Past research indicates that a dominant ethnic group has only one set of cultural schema, on which they base their judgments of all other groups (Aaker et al., 2000; Brumbaugh, 2002; S. A. Grier & Brumbaugh, 1999). Others have noted that there may be an accurate view [e.g. sociotype, (Triandis, 1994)], inaccurate view [e.g. stereotype, (Katz & Braly, 1933)], or a combination of the two views (Aaker et al., 2000; Brumbaugh, 2002; S. A. Grier & Brumbaugh, 1999) of the non-dominant group by the dominant group that may affect how they react to such stimuli. The findings here suggest that the dominant group has a sociotypical view of Iban and a stereotypical view of Chinese. The results of tests for the previous propositions also suggest that Malay respondents are more socially close to Iban rather than Chinese.

This again raises questions about distinctiveness theory. In this instance, Malay respondents indicate that there is no significant difference in their attitudes and behavioral intentions when the advertisement is in the Iban language compared to the Malay language. The ethnic cues in the Iban language advertisement were not enough to create a negative reaction, unlike the Chinese language advertisement. This suggests that social closeness/distance of the target group to Malay is more as a result of distinctiveness salience than just the numerical status of the non-dominant group.

Another interesting issue is the preference for the language used in the advertisements. Previous research has suggested that bilinguals process advertisements better in their first language than their second (D. Luna & Peracchio,

2001) and prefer advertisements in their first language (Gerritsen et al., 2000; Hernandez & Newman, 1992; Nicholls & Roslow, 1999; Wierzbicka, 1985a, 1985b). This is partly true here, where Malay respondents preferred the advertisement in their own language rather than Chinese. However, there was no difference in their reaction to the Iban language advertisement, apart from a limited, emotional (alienation) reaction. This suggest that marketers may target non-dominant groups that are close to the dominant group without losing potential sales from the dominant group and vice versa.

As with the findings for Proposition 1, the results for Proposition 3 (dominant group) raises questions about the efficacy of targeting non-dominant groups that are socially distinct from the majority ethnic group. However, the findings also suggest that if promotional efforts were targeted to a non-dominant group that is socially close and accepted by the dominant group, there are likely to be few negative reactions by the dominant group. This indicates that marketers should be aware of the social closeness/distance between groups in a society before targeting specific ethnic groups, otherwise the firm risks losing potential sales to the dominant group.

Theoretical Discussion for Non-Dominant Ethnic Group

This research aims to determine the reactions of those not targeted (in this instance non-dominant ethnic groups) to targeted advertisements. This is further investigated by noting the reactions of readers to advertisements that are perceived as novel as compared to a standard advertisement. This is investigated through the assessment of four responses, namely emotional reactions, attitude to the advertisement, attitude to the company and behavioral intentions.

The findings again raise the issue of language preference. Past research on bilinguals has shown that they prefer their own language (Gerritsen et al., 2000; Hernandez & Newman, 1992; Nicholls & Roslow, 1999; Wierzbicka, 1985a, 1985b), that they process it better and have different structures for each of the languages that they know (D. Luna & Peracchio, 2001; D. Luna & Peracchio, 2002). The findings suggest no strong differences in the non-dominant ethnic group's reaction to the advertisement in their own language compared to the dominant language advertisement. It could be that the non-dominant group used their knowledge of the dominant group cultural schema and rejected their own language advertisement (Aaker et al., 2000; Brumbaugh, 2002; S. A. Grier & Brumbaugh, 1999). This suggests that advertising campaigns to non-dominant groups could also utilize the dominant group language without causing negative reactions.

However, when the accommodated group is another non-dominant group, the reactions may differ. Although the Chinese reacted indifferently to the Iban language advertisement, the Iban reacted negatively to the Chinese language advertisement. Non-dominant groups have knowledge of their own group's and the dominant group cultural schema (Aaker et al., 2000; Brumbaugh, 2002; S. A. Grier & Brumbaugh, 1999). Reactions to other groups will be based on self-referencing and whatever limited knowledge of the other non-dominant group that they have. The findings suggest that Iban respondents referenced themselves with Malay and reacted as such. The Chinese respondents were indifferent (tended to be negative) to the Iban language advertisement suggesting that they did not reference themselves to the Malay or had limited knowledge of the Iban. This indicates that promotional activities that target non-dominant groups must also take into account the knowledge that other non-targeted, non-dominant groups have of them, their closeness/distance to the dominant group and their choice of reference.

However, the findings question the need to always incorporate elements into promotional activity that refer to the targeted group's culture (Hecht et al., 1993). Neither the Iban nor the Chinese appeared to like /dislike (the findings indicated differences were not significant) the novel advertisements in their own language any more than the standard (Malay language) advertisement. Nonetheless, Iban reactions tended to be negative while Chinese tended to be more positive, towards their own language advertisement. This suggests that Iban may have language related inferiority complex as well as being integrated into the dominant group (Koslow et al., 1994). The Chinese have a more positive language related complex due to the continuing use of Chinese in Chinese language schools and regular informal use (J. Platt, 1981; Watson, 1980a).

The findings also raise questions about international advertising theory and practice. Adaptation can occur for the creative selling proposition, elements in the advertisement and/or the language used (Harris, 1994). Previous studies also suggest that targeted respondents prefer their own language and fully adapted advertisements (Ueltschy & Ryans Jr., 1997). As the findings indicate, if the language is not the dominant group's language, there is a possibility of negative reactions from the dominant as well as non-dominant groups not targeted. If an advertisement is in a non-dominant group's language, the reaction of non-targeted (non-dominant) groups will depend on the social closeness/distance between the groups. This suggests that before international marketers adapt any advertisement through the use of language, they must first consider the cultural and social factors that might influence the targeted and non-targeted group's reactions.

Theoretical Discussion for Within Group Differences

The aim of Proposition four was to assess within-groups differences, based on ethnic identification strength.

Ethnic identity is a concept that is answered by the questions "What am I?" and "What am I not?" (Aboud & Christian, 1979; Brand et al., 1974; Dashefsky & Shapiro, 1974; Frideres & Goldenberg, 1982). This refers to identification with a group (Dashefsky & Shapiro, 1974; Driedger, 1978). Identification strength in this research is measured through language, friendship networks, religious affiliation, participation in clubs and organizations, endogamy, food preference and traditional celebrations (Driedger, 1975; Phinney, 1990; D. A. Rosenthal & Feldman, 1992).

A weak ethnic identifier (i.e. someone who identifies weakly with a particular culture or group) will have a different "What am I?" compared with a strong ethnic identifier. This difference means that the shared cultural schema of the ethnic group varies between the strong and the weak identifiers. The research does not ask to which worldview the groups subscribe, as theory is explicit in stating that the dominant group will only have its own worldview and that the non-dominant group will have its own plus other cultural group schemas they are aware of (Brumbaugh, 2002).

Previous studies about ethnic identification strength indicate that there are differences between individuals in the varying levels of ethnic affiliation and reactions to different stimuli (Alba & Chamlin, 1983; Christian et al., 1976; Deshpande et al., 1986; Donthu & Cherian, 1994; Gao et al., 1994). These differences have been depicted in previous studies about reactions to in-group vitality (Gao et al., 1994), shopping (Donthu & Cherian, 1994), consumption behavior (Deshpande et al., 1986) and advertisements (Appiah, 2001; C. I. Green, 1999; Simpson, Snuggs, Christiansen, & Simples, 2000).

However, the findings for this proposition indicate largely similar reactions by both weak and strong ethnic identifiers. This is contrary to the extant literature. A possible explanation is that this may be due to the social context in Malaysia, as well as to wide access to different language advertisements. Most of the previous studies looked at Hispanics in the USA where the social context may not be similar to Malaysia. This difference in social context and the ready access to (and familiarity with) different language advertisements in Malaysia, may result in less variability in intra group reactions. Management should consider this strong intra group cohesion in planning promotional activities. The findings also suggest that there are limited possibilities for sub-segmenting these ethnic groups.

Theoretical Discussion for between Group Differences

The lack of significant main interactions is puzzling, given previous studies (Bogardus, 1967; Fagan & O'Neill, 1965; P. R. Kunz & Oheneba-Sakyi, 1989; Lambert & Taylor, 1990; Payne Jr. et al., 1974) that have used the social distance scale used in this research (Bogardus, 1925) to assess how socially similar, or dissimilar, different ethnic groups are. Close examination of the scale suggests that it may not be a good measure for space between groups, particularly in this context. The scale may not necessarily be discrete (i.e. an interval scale) but categories (Churchill Jr., 2001). Treating this scale as an interval scale (even though it has been by many researchers) may not be valid, nor may dividing it into two strong or weak groups. This is because the statements used may not be seen as discrete points along a continuum. The findings here raise serious questions about the validity of the results reported by other authors who have used this scale and this is further discussed in the limitations' section in Chapter Nine.

Managerial Implications

The research has led to the development of a modified research model (refer to Figure 7 in Chapter Seven) to assess the likely reactions of targeted and non-targeted groups. The results suggest that targeting a specific ethnic group may not be a sustainable practice, as more and more neutral, or potential consumers, from other ethnic groups may see the targeted promotional activity and react negatively to it. The findings thus introduce a cautionary note, suggesting that managers would do well to consider the unintended damage that their targeted promotional practices have on the company in the long run. Management should also consider utilizing path dependencies for their current targeting decisions.

This research aims to provide a holistic view of the reactions of non-targeted groups to ethnically targeted advertising. The findings indicate that there are different levels of reaction, depending on the group being targeted and the relationship between the non-targeted and targeted groups. If a company targets a non-dominant group that is similar to the dominant ethnic group, there is a possibility of extending the segment to include the dominant group. This could be achieved by adding specific cues that relate to the dominant group, in promotional activities aimed at the non-dominant target group. If a company targets a non-dominant ethnic group that is dissimilar to the dominant group, there is a possibility of strong negative reactions from the dominant group. Management could reduce negative impacts on the company by using separate brands for different segments; an example of this is Toyota, which has a separate sub-brand for its second hand car market (Signature Class).

The findings indicate that if a company targets a dominant group, there is less likelihood of negative reactions from non-targeted (non-dominant) groups. The findings also suggest that a "middle ground" advertisement (that has both the dominant and non-dominant languages) may create positive emotional reactions from non-dominant groups. However, this may also be context specific and would require pre-testing in other market constructs.

The findings also suggest that there are at least two levels of negative reaction. The first is emotional and does not translate into attitudinal and behavioral negativity. The second is a negative reaction that includes emotional, attitudinal and behavioral responses. This is dependent on the targeted group. Management should therefore be aware of how groups construct their worldviews and the links (if any) between affective responses, cognition, attitudes and behavior. This is a deeper level of market research that not many firms engage in before selecting target markets.

The findings suggest that management should not have a myopic view of the market and only consider those targeted, as there are possible negative reactions to the company from those not targeted. A modified research model to assess the likely reactions of targeted and non-targeted groups is presented in Chapter Nine (refer to Figure 7) for management to utilize in their decision-making.

This research challenges the general assumption that different ethnic groups within a nation should always be addressed in their own language when being targeted by advertisers. Although the findings are context specific, managers should consider this issue before targeting ethnic segments. If the non-dominant group is indifferent to the use of the dominant group's language, then it could be considered for inclusion in targeted advertisements. This would in effect enlarge the market segment and should reduce negative reactions by non-target groups (particularly by the dominant group).

From an international advertising perspective, management should consider the use of the dominant ethnic group's language when crossing borders. International marketers should note the impact of the dominant language and its acceptance/rejection by non-dominant groups, before adapting or standardizing advertisements in new country markets. The findings suggest that this should reduce the likelihood of negative reactions from those groups, which are not targeted. However, management should also take into consideration the social and cultural context, the knowledge of the targeted group about other groups and vice versa, cultural similarity, distinctiveness issues and dominance.

The research also provides support for the social context view of distinctiveness theory. This suggests that defining a segment by ethnicity alone is not sufficient, as this may not preclude members of one ethnic group behaving like another. The findings show that Iban act as Malay, even though they consider themselves to be ethnically distinct. On the other hand, the dominant group (Malay) reacted much more positively to the Iban advertisements than to the Chinese advertisements.

Another context specific issue for management to consider is ethnic identification strength. Previous studies indicated that there should be differences between weak and strong ethnic identifiers. However, this research did not find such a relationship.

7. CONCLUSIONS, LIMITATIONS AND FURTHER RESEARCH

Conclusions

The research set out to examine the unintended effects of ethnically targeted advertising arising from negative reactions of those not targeted. Reactions that were assessed were emotions, attitude to the advertisement, attitude to the company and behavioral intentions. Five propositions were tested.

Proposition one posited that non-targeted groups would react more negatively to a targeted advertisement than would the targeted group. The findings indicate widespread negative emotional reactions among non-targeted ethnic groups. Negative attitudinal and behavioral reactions tended to be limited to one of the three ethnic groups targeted (i.e. the Chinese language advertisements). The findings also suggest that reactions are mitigated by ethnic dominance and the social context of the study.

Proposition two posited that there would be a direct (linear) relationship between the levels of accommodation and the strength of the reactions of non-targeted groups. The findings identify few differences in reactions to advertisements with high and low levels of accommodation to targeted groups. The findings instead suggest that there may be a curvilinear reaction to language accommodation attempts. In other words, non-targeted groups appeared to prefer advertisements that occupied the 'middle ground' of the speech accommodation continuum (i.e. those advertisements that used a mixture of dominant and non-dominant group languages).

Proposition three posited that novel language advertisements would generate stronger negative responses than standard language advertisements by those not targeted. The findings suggest that there is a strong preference for the standard language advertisement compared to a novel language advertisement. However, this is mitigated by the dominance of the ethnic group, ethnic distinctiveness and the social context.

Proposition four posited that there will be within group differences in reactions to fully targeted (accommodated) advertisements, depending how strongly readers identify with a particular ethnic group. The findings indicate few differences in reactions by weak and strong ethnic identifiers. The significant differences that did occur were limited to emotional reactions.

Proposition five posited that there would be between group differences in reactions to targeted advertisements, depending on the social distance between groups. The MANOVA test result indicated no significant interactions between the factors studied and so no further analysis was carried out in this area.

Contributions of the Study

The objective of this research is to test propositions related to how those not targeted would react to ethnically targeted advertisements. A secondary objective was to extend the research from the unintended effects of targeted advertising to impacts on the company, a significant move away from the social and moral issues studied in the past. Previous studies have tended to suggest that attitudes and behavioral intentions are important predictors of advertising effectiveness, while emotions have been shown to play an important role in consumer behavior.

The reactions of non-targeted groups that view targeted advertisements may not seem an important issue to many marketing academics and practitioners and has generally been neglected by scholars. Nevertheless, previous studies have shown that unintended audiences often view an advertisement targeted at other groups and make decisions regarding the advertisement, brand and company behind the advertising. These decisions may affect future consumer behavior. Previous work by Ehrenberg and associates show that consumers are polygamous in their choice of brands. Thus, this research seeks to significantly add to the body of marketing knowledge about the unintended effects of targeted advertising. The sample for the main study consisted of representatives from three ethnic groups in Malaysia, which is an ethnically plural society and therefore an appropriate context for cross-cultural marketing research. The findings contribute not only to marketing theory but also to other theories used to operationalize the research (e.g. SAT, Distinctiveness Theory and Cultural Schema).

This research extends previous targeting knowledge by showing that:

1. There are likely to be negative emotional reactions to targeted advertising by those not targeted. Evidence for negative attitudes towards the advertisement, attitudes towards the company and behavioral intentions tend to be limited.
2. These negative reactions appear to be mediated by ethnic dominance, knowledge of the targeted group, perceived similarity or difference, as well as the social and cultural context.
3. There is a need for a holistic approach to assessing the efficacy of targeting instead of the present myopic view, which tends to focus only on benefits and ignores potential negative effects. The research provides a revised research model (refer to Figure 7) that management can use in the strategic planning of promotional and marketing activity before, during and after implementing a targeted promotional plan.

This research also extends current knowledge about three language and culture theories used to operationalize the research:

1. SAT. The findings suggest that there are limits to the use of this theory in a marketing perspective. Instead of the expected linear relationships between strength of readers' reactions and levels of language accommodation, the findings also provide for a curvilinear relationship;
2. Distinctiveness Theory. The findings suggest that distinctiveness may be affected more by the social context than the numerical strength of an ethnic group. The results also suggest that researchers should be cautious about presupposing that people who identify with different ethnic groups will necessarily react in different

ways to a given set of stimuli. From a marketing perspective, this also raises questions about the usefulness of ethnicity as a basis for segmentation;

3. Cultural Schema. The findings indicate that the dominant group in Malaysia reacts differently to the two non-dominant groups (Iban and Chinese), suggesting that the constructs of a dominant group's worldview may not be limited to a single set of cultural schema;

4. Social Distance. The findings suggest that there are questions about the validity of this commonly used scale.

Revised Model

The initial research model (refer to Figure 1) guided the tests of the propositions in this research. The author has revised the initial model in the light of the findings, to help guide future research into the effects (positive and negative) of targeted advertising (refer to Figure 7)

The model takes into account the positive or negative reactions of the targeted and non-targeted segments. This is measured by emotional, attitudinal and behavioral intentions responses. The variables can be weighted from a company viewpoint (based on experience, research and company plans) and/or the consumer viewpoint (based on expectation, beliefs and attitudes). Responses can be weighted according to the size of segments. Net outcomes can then be decided by utilizing a multi attribute assessment table (refer to Table 16).

Figure 7 Modified Model to Guide Future Research Into the Likely Effects of Targeted Advertising

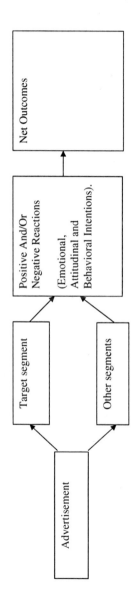

Table 16 Sample of Multi Attribute Assesment Table for Segment Comparison

Response / Segments*	Emotional	Attitudinal	Behavioral Intentions
Segment 1	X	X	X
Segment 2	X	X	X
Segment...n	X	X	X
Net Outcome	XX	XX	XX

* Note – responses can be weighted according to the size of segment and/or relative importance of variables according to company and/or consumer perspectives.

Limitations of the Research

The limitations of the research can be considered from two main perspectives; the first is the context used to test the propositions; the second is the method. The findings in the research must be seen in the light of these limitations.

From a contextual point of view, Malaysia is a plural society (Furnivall, 1948) and not a melting pot of ethnic groups. This plural society allows for the creation of ethnic groups' own cultural schema that are used to judge the advertisements. Nevertheless, there is a push from the government to integrate ethnic groups into the dominant group (Joseph & Holden, 2001). This is achieved through by education and integration activities (Watson, 1980b). This may have affected respondents' reactions to the advertisements that they saw.

Iban respondents appear to be quite well integrated into the dominant culture judging by their reaction to the advertisements, language and lifestyle (Noriah, 1994; Postill, 1999; Tawai, 1997). The Chinese, on the other hand, are still clearly different from the Malays in the nature of their language and culture (Andaya & Andaya, 1982; K. H. Lee & Tan, 2000; J. Platt, 1981). Chinese numbers are large enough to withstand the distinct push from Government for integration (Jabatan Perangkaan Malaysia, 1999) which means that they are still relatively distinct and most likely to judge and react to advertisements on a different level than the Malay or Iban respondents.

The research is limited to three ethnic groups. It does not take into consideration the impact of those who consider themselves to be a mix of the races or who have become acculturated into the dominant culture. This includes people such as the 'Baba Nyonya' who are Chinese, but whose lifestyle is integrated into the Malay lifestyle or those who have become Malay by law, because of their change in religion. As Malay, Chinese and Iban are the focus of the research, it limits the generalization of the findings to other ethnic groups and other country markets.

The research uses ethnic targeting. This limits the discussion and the generalizability of the findings to how ethnic groups in Malaysia react to a targeted effort. It does not analyze reactions of demographic or psychographic groups. Therefore, the generalizability of the findings is again limited. A more fundamental issue is whether ethnicity is a valid basis for segmentation at all, given the results discussed under propositions four and five.

The possible influence that attitudes towards other groups (e.g. stereotype, sociotype and aspirations) might have on reactions to the advertisements was also not assessed. Were the negative reactions based on attitudes towards the other group or just the advertisement? The research tried to take this into account by measuring social distance between the groups, but the scale used to measure social distance appears to be questionable.

Method used
A clear limitation of the research method is that it measures accommodation by varying the language used in the advertisements, but with a similar background for all advertisements. A different background for each advertisement might have projected full accommodation. However, this would have necessitated testing a much larger number of advertisements, a large factorial design and a much larger sample (the sample size is already large, with 1173 respondents). The basis for such a background change would also have been questionable. Following pre-testing, it was decided to only change the language, in keeping with the literature on language continuum (Roslow & Nicholls, 1996) and accommodation theory (H. Giles et al., 1973) as discussed in Chapter Three. Besides, pre-testing of a wider number of advertisements from which the final five to be tested were chosen, indicated that the proxy advertisements (Chinese language with Iban background for targeting Chinese and Malay language with Iban background for targeting Malay) were perceived to be targeted at Chinese or Malay segments respectively.

There is a question regarding the novelty of the propositions, as they sound all very familiar, to those from previous research investigating ethnic targeting (Koslow et al., 1994; Touchstone et al., 1999), accommodation (H. Giles et al., 1973; H. Giles et al., 1976; Simard et al., 1976) and dominance (Brumbaugh, 2002). However, the novelty does not lie just in the context of the main study, but more in the issue studied, which is the reactions of non-targeted groups to targeted advertisements. By using the context of ethnicity, these propositions have to be looked into through the lenses of ethnic studies, while questioning the responses of those not targeted. Further studies have to be carried out in different contexts, such as along different demographic or psychographic groups, in order to test the generalizability of the reactions. An example would be the issue of the relative dominance of targeted and non-targeted groups. The research utilizes a number of previous studies as its base (Aaker et al., 2000; Brumbaugh, 2002; S. A. Grier & Brumbaugh, 1999). If the context were to be demographics, dominance issues may be limited to numerical considerations and/or other aspects of dominance, such as opinion leadership.

Although the researcher took great care in obtaining a favorable response rate (74%), the use of a convenience sample and inability to conduct non-response bias checks are limitations and limit the generalizability of the findings. However, this may not be a serious problem in an exploratory study such as this.

The use of government officials in the role of interviewer may have created opportunities for bias in the responses. This may especially be true in the first phase of data collection where the Ministry of Unity officials were involved in gathering data. Respondents may have wanted to please the officials and be seen to be providing socially desirable answers, therefore reducing the impact of questions such as emotional reaction, alienation, racism and other similarly emotionally laden questions.

The second phase of data collection also created opportunities for possible bias when the enumerators read the questions to respondents. Direct contact with the enumerator and lack of privacy, may have resulted in some interviewer bias as well as some social desirability bias. However, the results suggest otherwise. There were clear qualitative statements of dislike for advertisements such as "Don't like because this advertisement is racist. Looks like it emphasizes only Iban, even though the background is more Malay. I am not confident of this advertisement (D016, F, 20, S, M, 6, 4)." The quantitative findings also indicate negative emotional reactions, alienation, racism and other similar emotionally laden questions.

Another limitation of any quantitative study is the meaning of the magnitude of difference when data is significant. Does the 0.7 or 1.7 difference in mean response to questions on a scale of one to seven have a clear meaning in the real world? The findings have been through a rigorous statistical analysis and yet these differences in magnitude are clearly only a numerical expression of difference. However, the qualitative findings seem to lend weight to the conclusion that the magnitudes of the differences in responses between groups are viable and significant. The qualitative responses are presented in conjunction with the statistical findings in Chapter Eight and in Appendix 1.

The research used five different advertisements, but each respondent only saw one. There was no opportunity for a direct comparison of advertisements by each individual, as this would necessitate an extremely long questionnaire. Because there was no comparison, individual reactions was clearly for that one advertisement alone. However, the issue of homogeneity of groups were also assessed and discussed in Chapter Six in order to obtain meaningful comparisons of the views of different groups of respondents.

The randomization of the measurement scale items used in the questionnaire may have also resulted in a lower score for some questions. This was because each variable studied was not presented *en masse* but separately and randomly. A similar situation and finding was also reported by (Touchstone et al., 1999). This may have lessened the impact of the reactions for the variables studied.

The research also tested each and every item used in each scale for invariance across the three groups. By doing so, there were a number of items that were deleted from the measurement scales, resulting in a smaller grouping of questions for each variable. This therefore means that the variables discussed cannot be seen as identical to previous studies. However, as shown in Chapter Six, the variance expressed by these variables is similar or higher than that reported in previous studies, indicating a good description of the variables studied.

Some questions may have been too blatant for Malaysian respondents especially those relating to anger, threat and racism. Respondents may not want to be seen as racist, for example, which may have led to some degree of concealment as to the strength of their real views (Touchstone et al., 1999).

Social distance measures the distance between identified ethnic groups. A number of reasons are offered as to why this scale did not work:

1. The distance measured in the scale may not relate to discrete points along a continuum (i.e. an interval scale) but categories (Weinfurt and Moghaddam, 2001;Bjerke and Al-Meer, 1993). Therefore, dividing these into groups of weak or strong may not be valid either;
2. Treating this scale as an interval scale may not be valid, even though it has been used in this way by other researchers;
3. It is a scale created from the perspective of a dominant group and may not work outside that dominant group (Lee, Sapp, and Ray, 1996);
4. It is based on a Western hierarchy that may not apply to an Eastern culture (Hsu, 1983; Triandis, 1995;Weinfurt and Moghaddam, 2001);
5. The statements used are too direct and strong and could be viewed as racist. This seems to have resulted in a biased reaction by respondents (towards the least racist parts of the scale), as they appear to want to avoid being perceived as racist. A similar finding was reported by (Touchstone et al., 1999).

This suggests that previous research that used this scale also operationalized social distance in an erroneous manner. Others, who have used a Bogardus-type social distance scale to measure other forms of distance, may also have operationalized that distance in an erroneous manner.

Aside from social distance, the behavioral measures used in this research may be criticised. The use of behavioral (word-of-mouth and purchase intention) measures for a fictitious product creates doubt as to its external validity (as discussed in section 6.2.5). Perhaps a better method to measure behavior would be to incorporate a more probabilistic measure such as the Juster scale (Juster, 1966). The Juster scale can be used to determine behavioral measures in terms of probability and enable better prediction (Garland, 2002). More importantly, the Juster scale would be a better scale for further studies that intend to validate behavioral probabilities (Pickering & Isherwood, 1974). Nevertheless, it has been shown that there is high correlation between the Juster scale and behavioral intention scales (Gruber, 1970) as used in this study.

The use of standardized Likert Scales with a scale range of one to seven may also be criticised. As detailed in section 6.3 (Scale Development), there was a need in this study to standardize the 14 various scales to make it easier for respondents to answer the questions, as well as simplifying data analysis. This may have resulted in a larger spread of responses. It would be expected that the mean, median, or the centre value, would change proportionately. Researchers may use the seven point scales in a slightly different way to five point scales and the variances may also differ. However, the true relationship of the five with a sevenpoint would be unknown, but likely to be similar (Cox, 1980; Garland, 1991; Ramsay, 1973).

It must also be understood that most of the measures used in this study have been frequently used, tried and validated. Nevertheless, it is important, as in the case of the social distance scale discussed earlier, to not accept any scale at face value. An example would be the purchase intention scale, which has a statement that has two possible meanings. However, this statement was eliminated in the validity test.

The use of a fictitious advertisement, product and company may have also confounded the findings. For example, the advertisements had only a limited number of words. Some respondents could not tell if the product was a soft drink (as was intended) or alcohol and the company name was certainly not recognized. As a fast moving consumer good, a soft drink is a lower involvement product than a durable good. This could result in less cognitive effort by respondents and therefore more average responses to the statements provided. These factors may have contributed towards the like or dislike of the advertisement and subsequent positive or negative reactions measured in the study. Nevertheless, it was necessary, as the researcher did not want past associations with a product or company to interfere with the findings.

Findings from this research must be seen in the light of the context and methods used. The use of specific ethnicity, advertisements and methodology limits discussion and generalizations. However, the research has resulted in new findings and raises further areas that need to be explored.

Further Research

Further research resulting from the research can be broken down into two main areas: the first is the context used to test the propositions; the second, is to answer the methodological issues identified in the limitations.

There is a lack of replication research in marketing. One study found that replication research is generally endorsed in the sciences, but not so in the advertising/consumer behavior/marketing literature (Madden, Easley, & Dunn, 1995). This inhibits further understanding of issues highlighted and investigated in seminal works such as a doctorate degree.

The context used in this research is ethnic based targeting, and is therefore culturally influenced. There are two main limitations to this research; context and methodology as discussed earlier. These limitations can be overcome by further replications of the study in different cultural contexts in order to improve the generalizability of the findings.

A methodological issue raised here is that there is no direct comparison of advertisements by a single respondent. Further research could assess whether direct comparison of advertisements affect respondents' ratings when compared to the approach used by this research, in order to develop a better methodological approach in future, targeted advertising studies.

Other variables such as attitude towards other ethnic groups could also be incorporated into future ethnic targeting research. Given problems with the social distance scale used in this research, measures such as attitude towards other races (Albright, Kirsch, Lawshe, & Remmers, 1956; Kasheira & Smith, 1943; Remmers, 1934), or other specifically developed measures, may prove to be better at assessing distance between ethnic groups. Social similarity measures could also be developed to assess the differences in reactions of socially close and socially distant ethnic groups or indeed, other segments in targeted advertising.

Further studies could incorporate subtler measures for racism, anger and perceived threat. These measures could take into account subtle prejudices, stereotypes and sociotypes of these groups in a manner that is not threatening to respondents.

The nature of the product class could also be investigated. For example, it would be interesting to explore whether an ethnically biased product creates stronger reactions among those not targeted, than an ethnically neutral product. An ethnically biased product could be a high involvement purchase for a particular target group but a low involvement purchase for the non-targeted group. Alternatively, product class issues could be investigated, noting the impact of different products on unintended reactions.

The potential of additional variables, that were not included in this research, could also be investigated. For instance, researchers could consider cultural values and their impact on unintended reactions to targeted advertisements. For example, the cultural values of Chinese consumers' are likely to be different to Malay consumers' values.

The findings also indicate that there were limits to the theories used to operationalize the research, such as distinctiveness theory, accommodation theory and cultural schema. Further studies could look more closely at how each theory clarifies or confuses the debate about the influences of the effectiveness of ethnically targeted advertising.

Future studies could also use the modified model to assess the costs and benefits of targeted advertising, by adding the positive and negative reactions of targeted and non-targeted audiences of mass media advertising. This could be replicated for various types of media.

Further studies could also look into the possibility of removing affective measures totally. Instead, they could focus solely on behavioral intentions incorporating the Juster Scale (Juster, 1966). The Juster scale can be used to estimate the demand – advertisement relationship (Gruber, 1970). This can be tested via a real life product and advertisement in order to determine the potential probability of purchasing or not purchasing, the product and its impact on the company's sales. This behavior could then be validated in a post test. Other studies could incorporate the use of the Juster scale to better understand the relationship between Word-of-Mouth and purchase intention.

Ehrenberg's finding that many product users are polygamous and that, rather than be brand switchers, actually have several brands in their product category set, could be extended to future research of intended and unintended advertisement audiences' reactions.

This research acts as the starting point for developing a more holistic view of the unintended effects of targeted advertising. Unfortunately, it is limited by its scope. Further replications of the research could look at applying the revised research model to other marketing contexts, such as the unintended effects of targeting advertisements at particular demographic or psychographic segments

Further studies could be carried out using real advertisements to assess overall costs and benefits. For example, in Malaysia, advertisements for Guinness Malta use

English, Malay, Chinese, Malay and Chinese, or Malay, Chinese and English language in separate advertisements and promotional tools (refer Appendix 2). On the downside though, it may be more difficult to control for company, brand and product influences. The modified model may be used to assess overall costs and benefits of real advertisements.

There is also limited research into the magnitude of the reactions of those not targeted. Companies are currently being exhorted to target ethnic groups, without being aware that they risk current or future losses from those not targeted. Further research could extend the current findings of negative reactions from those not targeted to measuring dependent variables of direct important area to a company, such as market share, share holder value, share of voice in the market, positive top of mind awareness, company image and sales. Using the modified model may help to carry out this research.

Reference

Aaker, J. L., Brumbaugh, A. M., & Grier, S. A. (2000). Non-target Market Effects and Viewer Distinctiveness: The Impact of Target Marketing on Attitudes. *Journal of Consumer Psychology, 9*(3), 127 - 140.

Aboud, F. E., & Christian, J. (1979). Development of Ethnic Identity. In L. Eckensberger, Y. Poortinga & W. J. Lonner (Eds.), *Cross-cultural contributions to psychology.* Lisse: Swets and Zeitlinger.

Abraham, S. J. (1999, 2 - 4 August). *National Identity and Ethnicity: Malaysian Perspectives.* Paper presented at the International Malaysian Studies Conference, Universiti Malaya, Kuala Lumpur.

ACTR. (1990). *Advertising Code for Television and Radio.* Kuala Lumpur: Ministry of Information.

Adnan, H. (1994). *Advertising in Malaysia.* Malaysia: Pelanduk Publications.

Agrawal, M. (1995). Review of a 40-year Debate in International Advertising. *International Marketing Review, 12*(1), 26 - 49.

Akerlof, G. A. (1997). Social Distance and Social Decisions. *Econometrica, 65*(5), 1005 - 1027.

Alba, R. D., & Chamlin, M. (1983). Ethnic Identification Among Whites. *American Sociological Review, 48*(April), 240 - 247.

Alba, R. D., & Moore, G. (1982). Ethnicity in the American Elite. *American Psychological Review, 47*(June), 373 - 382.

Albaum, G., & Tse, D. K. (2001). Adaptation of International Marketing Strategy Components, Competitive Advantage, and Firm Performance: A Study of Hong Kong Exporters. *Journal of International Marketing, 9*(4), 59 - 81.

Albright, L. E., Kirsch, A. D., Lawshe, C. H., & Remmers, H. H. (1956). A Longitudinal Comparison of Student Attitudes Towards Minorities. *Journal of Educational Psychology, 47,* 372 - 379.

Allport, G. (1954). *The Nature of Prejudice*: Doubleday.

Andaya, B. W., & Andaya, L. Y. (1982). *A History Of Malaysia.* London: Macmillan Education Ltd.

Andreasen, A. R. (1990). Cultural Interpretation: A Critical Consumer Research Issue for the 1990's. In M. E. Goldberg, G. Gorn & R. W. Pollay (Eds.), *Advances in Consumer Research* (Vol. 17, pp. 847 - 849). Provo, UT: Association for Consumer Research.

Annan, F. (1999). *Does Participation in Sponsorship Improve Corporate Image?* University of Otago, Dunedin.

Anonymous. (1999, Jul 5). Anti-smoking Ads for Vietnamese-Americans. *Marketing News, 33,* 4.

Anonymous. (2000). *The Chinese of Malaysia.* Retrieved 24 Nov, 2003, from http://www.bebeyond.com/LearnEnglish/BeAD/Readings/DiasporaMalaysia.html

Anonymous. (2001a). Asiaweek: The Nations: Malaysia: 'When You Grow Old, You Face Reality'. *Asiaweek,* 1.

Anonymous. (2001b). *What it's All About.* Retrieved 10 December, 2001, from http://www.iol.ie/~anansi/about.htm

Anonymous. (2002, Dec 19). Racial Integration Key To National Stability, Says Mahathir. *Bernama,* p. 1.

Anonymous. (2004). *Press Statement: Population Distribution And Basic Demographic Characteristics Report. Population And Housing Census 2000.*

Retrieved 12 June, 2004, from
http://www.statistics.gov.my/English/pressdemo.htm

Anschuetz, N. (2002). Why a Brand's Most Valuable Consumer is the Next One it Adds. *Journal of Advertising Research, 42*(1), 15 - 21.

Appiah, O. (2001). Ethnic Identification on Adolescents' Evaluation of Advertisements. *Journal of Advertising Research, 41*(5), 7 - 22.

Appleman, R., & Muysken, P. (1987). *Language Contact and Bilingualism.* Great Britain: Edward Arnold.

Argandona, A. (1998). The Stakeholder Theory and the Common Good. *Journal of Business Ethics, 17*(9/10), 1093 - 1103.

Armstrong, K. L. (1999). Nike's communication with Black Audiences: A Sociological Analysis of Advertising Effectiveness via Symbolic Interactionism. *Journal of Sport and Social Issues, 23*(3), 266 - 286.

Asmah, H. O. (1977). *The Phonological Diversity of the Malay Dialects.* Kuala Lumpur: Dewan Bahasa Dan Pustaka.

Asmah, O. (1983). *The Malay People Of Malaysia And Their Languages.* Kuala Lumpur: Dewan Bahasa Dan Pustaka.

Asp, K. (1986). *Maktiga Massmedier.* Stockholm: Academic Literature.

Bagozzi, R. P. (1994). Measurement in Marketing Research. In R. P. Bagozzi (Ed.), *Principles of Marketing Research.* Oxford, UK: Blackwell Business.

Ball, P., Giles, H., Byrne, J. L., & Berechree, P. (1984). Situational Constraints on the Evaluative Significance of Speech Accommodation. *International Journal of the Sociology of Language, 46*, 115 - 130.

Bargh, J. A. (1990). Auto-Motives: Preconscious Determinants of Social Interaction. In E. T. Higgins & R. M. Sorentino (Eds.), *Handbook of Motivation and Cognition: Foundation of Social Behavior* (Vol. 2). New York: The Guilford Press.

Barnard, N., & Ehrenberg, A. (1997). Advertising: Strongly Persuasive or Nudging? *Journal of Advertising Research, 37*(1), 21 - 31.

Barth, F. (1969). *Ethnic Groups and Boundaries: The Social Organization of Culture Difference.* London: Allen and Urwin.

Batra, R., & Ray, M. L. (1986). Affective Responses Mediating Acceptance of Advertising. *Journal of Consumer Research, 13*(September), 234 - 249.

Baum, T. (1996). Images of Tourism Past and Present. *International Journal of Contemporary Hospitality Management, 8*(4), 25 - 30.

Becker, B. W., & Kaldenberg, D. O. (2000). Factors Influencing the Recommendation of Nursing Homes. *Marketing Health Services, 20*(4), 22 - 28.

Bell, A. (1991). Audience Accommodation in the Mass Media. In H. Giles (Ed.), *Contexts of Accommodation: Developments in Applied Sociolinguistics* (pp. 69 - 102). Cambridge: Cambridge University Press.

Bennett, J. W. (1975). *The New Ethnicity: Perspectives from Ethnology.* St. Paul, MI: West Publishing Co.

Berger, A. A. (1995). *Essentials of Mass Communication Theory.* London: Sage Publications.

Bergier, M. J. (1986). Predictive Validity of Ethnic Identification Measures: An Illustration of the English-French Classifications Dilemma in Canada. *Academy of Marketing Science, 14*(2), 37 - 42.

Berry, J. W. (1980). Acculturation as Varieties of Adaptation. In A. M. Padilla (Ed.), *Acculturation: Theory, Models, and Some New Findings* (pp. 9 - 26). Boulder, CO: Westview.

Berry, J. W. (1990). Psychology of Acculturation. In J. J. Berman (Ed.), *Cross-cultural Perspectives: Proceedings of the Nebraska Symposium on Motivation* (pp. 201 - 234).

Bhat, S., Leigh, T. W., & Wardlow, D. L. (1998). The Effect of Consumer Prejudice on Ad Processing: Heterosexual Consumers' Responses to Homosexual Imagery in Ads. *Journal of Advertising, 27*(4), 9 - 28.

Bilous, F. R., & Krauss, R. M. (1988). Dominance and Accommodation in the Conversational Behaviour of Some and Mixed Gender Dyads. *Language and Communication, 8*, 183 - 194.

Bjerke, B., & Al-Meer, A. (1993). Culture's Consequences: Management in Saudi Arabia. *Leadership & Organization Development Journal, 14*(2), 30.

Bloomfield, L. (1933). *Language*. New York.

Bogardus, E. S. (1925). Measuring Social Distance. *Journal of Applied Sociology, 9*, 299 - 308.

Bogardus, E. S. (1967). *A Forty Year Racial Distance Study*. Pasadena: University of Southern California Press.

Bourhis, R. Y. (1991). Organizational Communication and Accommodation: Toward Some Conceptual and Empirical Links. In H. Giles (Ed.), *Contexts of Accommodation: Developments in Applied Sociolinguistics*. Cambridge: Cambridge University Press.

Brand, E. S., Ruiz, R. A., & Padilla, A. M. (1974). Ethnicity Identification and Preference: A Review. *Psychological Bulletin, 86*, 860 - 890.

Brewer, M. B. (1979). In-Group Bias in the Minimal Intergroup Situation: A Cognitive-Motivational Analysis. *Psychological Bulletin, 86*(2), 307 - 324.

Brewer, M. B. (1999). The Psychology of Prejudice: In-group Love or Out Group Hate? *The Journal of Social Issues, 55*(3), 429 - 444.

Brewer, M. B. (2001). In-group Identification and Inter-group Conflict: When Does In-group Love Become Out Group Hate? In R. Ashmore, L. Jussim & D. Wilder (Eds.), *Social Identity, Inter-group Conflict, and Conflict Reduction*. New York: Oxford University Press.

Brinkerhoff, M. B., & Jacob, J. C. (1994). Racial, Ethnic and Religious Social Distance in Surinam: An Exploration of the 'Strategic Alliance Hypothesis' in a Caribbean Community. *Ethnic and Racial Studies, 17*, 636 - 661.

Brouillard, J. (1983). Corporate Reputation Counts. *Advertising Age, 54*(48), M.

Brown, R., & Gaertner, S. (2001). *Blackwell Handbook of Social Psychology: Intergroup Processes*. Malden, MA: Blackwell.

Brumbaugh, A. M. (1995). *Managing Diversity: A Cultural Knowledge Approach To Communicating To Multiple Market Segments*. Unpublished PhD, Duke University.

Brumbaugh, A. M. (2002). Source and Nonsource Cues in Advertising and Their Effects on the Activation of Cultural and Subcultural Knowledge on the Route to Persuasion. *Journal of Consumer Research, 29*(2), 258 - 269.

Buck, A. (1998). Asian and Hispanic Markets Are Big Business in Houston. *Texas Banking, 87*(3), 22.

Buller, D., & Anne, R. (1992). The Effects of Speech Rate Similarity on Compliance. *Western Journal of Communication, 56*, 37 - 53.

Burke, K. (1969). *A Rhetoric of Motives*. Berkeley: University of California Press.

Burnam, M. A., Telles, C. A., Karno, M., Hough, R. L., & Escobar, J. I. (1987). Measurement of Acculturation in a Community Population of Mexican-Americans. *Hispanic Journal of Behavioral Sciences, 9*(2), 105 - 130.

Burton, D. (1996). Ethnicity and Consumer Financial Behavior: A Case Study of British Asians in the Pensions Market. *International Journal of Bank Marketing, 14*(7), 21 - 31.

Byrne, D. (1969). Attitudes and Attraction. *Advances in Experimental Social Psychology, 4*, 35 - 89.

Byrne, D. (1971). *The Attraction Paradigm.* New York: Academic Press.

Caetano, R. (1987). Acculturation and Drinking Patterns Among US Hispanics. *British Journal of Addiction, 82*, 789 - 799.

Cahill, D. J. (1997). Target Marketing and Segmentation: Valid and Useful Tools for Marketing. *Management Decision, 35*(1), 10 -.

Caltabiano, N. (1984). Perceived Differences in Ethnic Behavior: A Pilot Study of Italo-Australian Canberra Residents. *Psychological Reports, 5*, 867 - 873.

Camp, S. D., Saylor, W. G., & Wright, K. N. (2001). Racial Diversity of Correctional Workers and Inmates: Organizational Commitment, Teamwork, and Workers' Efficacy in Prisons. *Justice Quarterly, 18*(2), 411 - 427.

Cantwell, J. (2001, Dec 31). Chrysler Sets Up Asian-language Ads in Western Markets. *Automotive News, 76*, 8.

Carroll, J. B. (1963). Linguistic Relativity, Contrastive Linguistics, and Language Learning. *International Review of Applied Linguistics, 1*, 1 - 20.

Carroll, J. B., & Casagrande, J. B. (1958). The Function of Language Classifications in Behaviour. In E. E. Maccoby, T. Newcomb & E. L. Hartley (Eds.), *Readings in Social Psychology* (Vol. 3, pp. 18 - 31). New York: Holt, Rinehart, & Winston.

Cervantes, F. J. (1980). The Forgotten Consumer: The Mexican-American. In R. P. Bagozzi (Ed.), *1980 Educators' Proceedings* (pp. 180 - 183). Chicago: American Marketing Association.

Chai, H. C. (1971). *Education and Nation Building in Plural Societies: The West Malaysian Experience* (Monograph No. 6): Development Studies Centre. Australian National University.

Chaiken, S., & Maheswaran, D. (1994). Heuristic Processing Can Bias Systematic Processing: Effects of Source Credibility, Argument Ambiguity, and Task Importance on Attitude Judgment. *Journal of Personality and Social Psychology, 66*((March)), 460 - 473.

Chew, D. (1941). *Chinese Pioneers on the Sarawak Frontier 1841 - 1941.* London: Oxford University Press.

Christian, J., Gadfield, N. J., Giles, H., & Taylor, D. M. (1976). The Multidimensional and Dynamic Nature of Ethnic Identity. *International Journal of Psychology, 11*(4), 281 - 291.

Chudry, F., & Pallister, J. (2002). The importance of ethnicity as a segmentation criterion: The case of the Pakistani consumers' attitude towards direct mail compared with the indigenous population. *Journal of Consumer Behaviour, 2*(2), 125.

Churchill Jr., G. A. (1979). A Paradigm for Developing Better Measures of Marketing Constructs. *Journal of Marketing Research, 16*(1), 64.

Churchill Jr., G. A. (1983). *Marketing Research: Methodological Foundations* (3 ed.). Japan: Holt Saunders International Editions.

Churchill Jr., G. A. (1987). *Marketing Research. Methodological Foundations* (4 ed.). New York: Dryden Press.

Churchill Jr., G. A. (2001). *Basic Marketing Research.* USA: The Dryden Press.

Clark, H. H., & Clark, E. V. (1977). *Psychology and Language: An Introduction to Psycholinguistics*. San Diego, CA: Harcourt Brace Jovanovich.

Clarke, T. K. (1984). Situational Factors Affecting Preschoolers' Responses To Advertising. *Academy Of Marketing Science, 12*(4), 25 - 40.

Claycamp, H. J., & Massy, W. F. (1968). A Theory of Market Segmentation. *Journal of Marketing Research, November*, 388 - 394.

Collins, M. (1971). Market Segmentation - The Realities of Buyer Behavior. *Journal of the Market Research Society, 13*(3), 3.

Comstock, G., Chaffee, S., Katzman, N., McCombs, M., & Roberts, D. (1978). *Television and Human Behavior*. New York: Columbia University Press.

Connor, J. W. (1977). *Tradition and Change in Three Generation of Japanese American*. Chicago, IL: Nelson-Hall.

Constantinou, S. T., & Harvey, M. E. (1985). Dimensional Structure and Intergenerational Differences in Ethnicity: The Greek Americans. *Social Science Research, 69*(2), 235 - 254.

Cooper, J., & Lane, P. (1997). *Practical Marketing Planning*: Macmillan Business.

Corbett, E. (1965). *Classical Rhetoric for the Modern Student*. London: Oxford.

Cornwell, T. B. (1994). Advertising, Ethnicity and Attendance at the Performance Arts. *Journal of Professional Service Marketing, 10*(2), 145 - 157.

Corrigan, P. W., Edwards, A. B., Green, A., Diwan, S. L., & Penn, D. L. (2001). Prejudice, Social Distance, and Familiarity With Mental Illness. *Schizophrenia Bulletin, 27*(2), 219.

Coupland, N., Coupland, J., Giles, H., & Henwood, K. (1988). Accommodating the Elderly: Invoking and Extending a Theory. *Language in Society, 17*(1), 1 - 41.

Cox, E. P. (1980). The Optimal Number of Response Alternatives for a Scale: A Review. *Journal of Marketing Research, 17*(November), 407 - 422.

Crain, R. (2002). Unintended Results Haunt AT&T Wireless, Taco Bell. *Advertising Age, 73*, 15.

Crook, C. W., & Booth, R. (1997). Building Rapport in Electronic Mail Using Accommodation Theory. *SAM Advanced Management Journal, 62*(1), 4 - 17.

Csikszentmihalyi, M., & Beattie, O. V. (1979). Life Themes: A Theoretical and Empirical Exploration of Their Origins and Effects. *Journal of Humanistic Psychology, 19*(1), 45 - 63.

Cuellar, I., Harris, L. C., & Jasso, R. (1980). An Acculturation Scale for Mexican American Normal and Clinical Populations. *Hispanic Journal of Behavioral Sciences, 2*, 199 - 217.

Cui, G. (1997). Marketing Strategies in a Multi Ethnic Environment. *Journal of Marketing Theory and Practice, 5*(1), 122 - 134.

Dashefsky, A., & Shapiro, H. (1974). *Ethnic Identification Among American Jews: Socialization and Social Structure*. Lexington, MA: Lexington Books.

Davison, W. P. (1983). The Third-person Effect in Communication. *Public Opinion Quarterly, 47*, 1 - 15.

De Fleur, M. L., & Ball-Rokeach, S. (1982). *Theories of Mass Communication* (Vol. 4). New York: Longman.

Delener, N., & Neelankavil, J. P. (1990). Information Sources and Media Usage: A Comparison Between Asian and Hispanic Subcultures. *Journal of Advertising Research, 30*(3), 45.

Depret, E., & Fiske, S. (1993). Social Cognition and Power: Some Cognitive Consequences of Social Structure as a Source of Control Deprivation. In G.

Weary, F. Gleicher & K. Marsh (Eds.), *Control Motivation and Social Cognition* (Vol. 176 - 202). New York: Springer-Verlag.

Deschamps, J. (1982). Social Identity and Relations of Power Between Groups. In H. Tajfel (Ed.), *Social Identity and Inter-group Relations* (pp. 85 - 97). USA: Cambridge University Press.

Deshpande, R., Hoyer, W. D., & Donthu, N. (1986). The Intensity of Ethnic Affiliation: A Study of the Sociology of Hispanic Consumption. *Journal of Consumer Research, 13*, 214 - 220.

Deshpande, R., & Stayman, D. M. (1994). A Tale of Two Cities: Distinctive Theory and Advertising Effectiveness. *Journal of Marketing Research, 31*(1), 57.

Devito, J. A. (1986). *The Communication Handbook: A Dictionary.* Cambridge: Harper and Row.

Devos, G. (1975). Ethnic Pluralism: Conflict and Accommodation. In G. Devos & L. Romanucci-Ross (Eds.), *Ethnic identity: Cultural continuities and Change.* Palo Alto, CA: Mayfield.

Dickson, P. R. (1982). Person-Situation: Segmentation's Missing Link. *Journal of Marketing, 46*(Fall), 56 - 64.

Dicson, J. P., & MacLachlan, D. L. (1990). Social Distance and Shopping Behavior. *Academy of Marketing Science, 18*(1), 153 - 161.

Dijkstra, S., Geuijen, K., & de Ruijter, A. (2001). Multiculturalism and Social Integration in Europe. *International Political Science Review, 22*(1), 55.

Dixon, J. A., Tredoux, C. G., Durrheim, K., & Foster, D. H. (1994). The Role of Speech Accommodation and Crime Type in Attribution of Guilt. *The Journal of Social Psychology, 134*(4), 465 - 472.

Dohrenwend, B., & Smith, R. J. (1962). Towards a Theory of Acculturation. *Southwestern Journal of Anthropology, 18*, 30 - 39.

Donthu, N., & Cherian, J. (1994). Impact of Strength of Ethnic Identification on Hispanic Shopping Behaviour. *Journal of Retailing, 70*(4), 383 - 393.

Doosje, B., Branscombe, N. R., Spears, R., & Manstead, A. S. R. (1998). Guilty by Association: When One's Group Has A Negative History. *Journal of Personality and Social Psychology, 75*, 872 - 886.

Douglas, S. P., & Win, Y. (1987). The Myth of Globalization. *Columbia Journal of World Business, 22*(4), 19 - 29.

Downs, A. C., & Harrison, S. K. (1985). Embracing Age Spots or Just Plain Ugly? Physical Attractiveness Stereotyping as an Instrument of Sexism on American Television Commercials. *Sex Roles, 13*(1/2), 9 - 19.

Driedger, L. (1975). In Search of Cultural Identity Factors: A Comparison of Ethnic Students. *Canadian Review of Sociology and Anthropology, 12*, 150 - 162.

Driedger, L. (1978). *The Canadian Ethnic Mosaic.* Toronto: McClelland and Steward.

Dunn, W. (1992). The Move toward Ethnic Marketing. *Nations Business, 80*(7), 39 - 41.

Dyer, J., Vedlitz, A., & Worchel, S. (1989). Social Distance Among Racial and Ethnic Groups in Texas: Some Demographic Correlates. *Social Science Quarterly, 70*(3), 607.

Edell, J. A., & Staelin, R. (1983). The Information Processing of Pictures in Print Advertisements. *Journal of Consumer Research, 10*, 45 - 61.

Edwards, J. R. (1985). *Language, Society, and Identity.* New York: Oxford.

Ehrenberg, A. (1988). *Repeat-Buying: Facts, Theory and Aplications.* London: Griffin.

Ehrenberg, A. (1993). Even the Social Sciences Have Laws. *Nature, 365*, 385.

Ehrenberg, A. (2001). Marketing: Romantic or Realistic. *Marketing Insights, Summer,* 40 - 42.

Ehrenberg, A., Barnard, N., & Scriven, J. (1997). Differentiation or Salience. *Journal of Advertising Research, (November / December),* 7 - 14.

Ehrenberg, A., & Goodhardt, G. J. (1978). *Market Segmentation.* New York, NY.: J. Walter Thompson.

Ehrenberg, A., Goodhardt, G. J., & Barwise, T. P. (1990). Double Jeopardy Revisited. *Journal of Marketing, 54*(July), 82 - 91.

Elkin, T. (1998, Aug 10). AT&T Augments Marketing Efforts Against Students, Ethnic Consumers. *Brandweek, 39,* 14.

Elliot, D. L., Hanzlik, J. R., & Gliner, J. A. (1992). Attitudes of Occupational Therapy Personnel Toward Therapists with Disabilities. *The Occupational Therapy Journal of Research, 12,* 259 - 277.

Esslemont, D. H. B., & Ward, T. (1989). The Stability of Segmentation Solutions in A Commercial Survey. *New Zealand Journal of Business, 11,* 89 - 95.

Fagan, J., & O'Neill, M. (1965). A Comparison of Social-distance Scores Among College Students Samples. *The Journal of Social Psychology, 66,* 281 - 290.

Faiza, T. C. (2001, 24 Oktober). *Aspek Undang-undang Dalam Perlaksanaan Bahasa Malaysia di Sektor Kerajaan Tempatan.* Paper presented at the Kolokium Pemantapan Penggunaan Bahasa Kebangsaan di Tempat Awam dan Papan Tanda, Kuching.

Federation of Malaya. (1956). *Report of the Education Committee.* Kuala Lumpur: Government Printers.

Federation of Malaysia. (1985). *The Fifth Malaysia Plan, 1986 - 1990.* Kuala Lumpur: Government Printers.

Feinberg, F. M., Krishna, A., & Zhang, Z. J. (2002). Do We Care What Others Get? A Behaviorist Approach to Targeted Promotions. *Journal of Marketing Research, 39*(3), 277 - 291.

Felix-Ortiz De La Garza, M., Newcomb, M. D., & Myers, H. F. (1995). Multidimensional Measure of Cultural Identity for Latino and Latina Adolescents. In A. M. Padilla (Ed.), *Hispanic Psychology: Critical Issues in Theory and Research* (pp. 26 - 42). Thousand Oaks, CA: Serge Publications.

Ferrara, K. (1991). Accommodation in Therapy. In H. Giles (Ed.), *Contexts of Accommodation: Developments in Applied Sociolinguistics.* Cambridge: Cambridge University Press.

Fishbein, M., & Ajzen, I. (1975). *Belief, Attitude, Intention and Behaviour.* Reading, MA: Addison-Wesley.

Fishman, J. A. (1977a). Language and Ethnicity. In H. Giles (Ed.), *Language, Ethnicity and Intergroup Relations.* London: Academic Press.

Fishman, J. A. (1977b). Language, Ethnicity, and Racism, *Georgetown University Roundtable on Language and Linguistics.*

Fitzpatrick, M., Mulac, A., & Dindia, K. (1995). Gender Preferential Language Use in Spouse and Stranger Interaction. *Journal of Language and Social Psychology, 14,* 18 - 39.

Forehand, M. R., & Deshpande, R. (2001). What We See Makes Us Who We Are: Priming Ethnic Self-awareness and Advertising Response. *Journal of Marketing Research, 38*(3), 336 - 348.

Foss, D. J., & Hakes, D. T. (1978). *Psycholinguistics: An Introduction to the Psychology of Language.* Englewood Cliffs, NJ: Prentice Hall.

Fost, D. (1990). California's Asian Market. *American Demographics, 12*(10), 34 - 37.

Fountain, H. (1999, Mar 30). Proof Positive That People See Colors With the Tongue. *New York Times*, p. F.5.

Francis, J. N. P. (1991). When in Rome? The Effects of Cultural Adaptation on Intercultural Business Negotiations. *Journal of International Business Studies, 22*(Third Quarter), 403 - 428.

Franco, J. N. (1983). An Acculturation Scale for Mexican-American Children. *The Journal of General Psychology, 108*, 175 - 181.

Frank, R., Massy, W. F., & Wind, Y. (1972). *Market Segmentation*. Englewood CLiffs, N.J.: Prentice Hall.

Freeman, D. (1981). *Some reflections on the nature of Iban society*. Canberra: Department of Anthropology, Research School of Pacific Studies, Australian National University.

Freeman, J. D. (1955). *Iban agriculture* (No. 18). London: Her Majesty's Stationery Office; Colonial Research Report.

Freeman, J. D. (1958). The Family System of the Iban of Borneo. In J. Goody (Ed.), *The Development Cycle in Domestic Groups* (pp. 15 - 52). Cambridge: University Press.

Freeman, K. M. (1992). Target Marketing: The Logic of it All. *The Journal of Consumer Marketing, 9*(3), 15 -.

Frideres, J., & Goldenberg, S. (1982). Ethnic Identity: Myth and Reality in Western Canada. *International Journal of Intercultural Relations, 6*, 137 - 151.

Furnivall, J. S. (1948). *Colonial Policy and Practice*: Cambridge University Press.

Gallois, C., & Callan, V. J. (1991). Interethnic Accommodation: The Role of Norms. In H. Giles (Ed.), *Contexts of Accommodation: Developments in Applied Sociolinguistics* (pp. 245 - 269). Cambridge: Cambridge University Press.

Gao, G., Schmidt, K. L., & Gudykunst, W. B. (1994). Strength of Ethnic Identity and Perceptions of Ethnolinguistic Vitality Among Mexican Americans. *Hispanic Journal of Behavioral Sciences, 16*(3), 332.

Garcia, J. A. (1982). Ethnicity and Chicanos: Measurement of Ethnic Identification, Identity, and Consciousness. *Hispanic Journal of Behavioral Sciences, 4*, 295 - 314.

Garcia, M., & Lega, L. (1979). Development of A Cuban Ethnic Identity Questionnaire. *Hispanic Journal of Behavioral Sciences, 1*, 247 - 261.

Gardner, M. P. (1985). Does Attitude to the Ad Affect Brand Attitude Under a Brand Evaluation Set? *Journal of Marketing Research, 22*(May), 192 - 198.

Garland, R. (1991). The Mid-Point on a Rating Scale: Is it Desirable? *Marketing Bulletin*(2), 66 - 70.

Garland, R. (2002). Estimating Customer Defection in Personal Retail Banking. *The INternational Journal of Bank Marketing, 20*(7), 317 - 324.

Gazdik, T. (1998, Feb 16). Chevrolet Expands Hispanic Ad Emphasis With New TV, Print Work. *Adweek (Midwest Edition), 39*, 5.

Gentry, J. W., Jun, S., & Tansuhaj, P. (1995). Consumer Acculturation Processes and Cultural Conflict. *Journal of Business Research, 32*, 129 - 139.

Gerbner, G., Gross, L., Morgan, M., & Signorielli, N. (1980). The Mainstreaming of America: Violence Profile No. 11. *Journal of Communication, 30*, 10 - 27.

Gerritsen, M., Korzilius, H., Van Meurs, F., & Gijsbers, I. (2000). English in Dutch Commercials: Not Understood and Not Appreciated. *Journal of Advertising Research, 40*(4), 17 - 31.

Giles, H. (1971). Ethnocentrism and the Evaluation of Accented Speech. *British Journal of Social and Clinical Psychology, 10*, 187 - 188(a).

Giles, H. (1977a). *Language, Ethnicity and Intergroup Relations*. London: Academic Press.

Giles, H. (1977b). The Social Context of Speech: A Social Psychological Perspective. *ITL: A Review of Applied Linguistics, 35*, 27 - 42.

Giles, H., Baker, S., & Fielding, G. (1975). Communication Length as a Behavioral Index of Accent Prejudice. *International Journal of the Sociology of Language, 6*, 73 - 81.

Giles, H., Bourhis, R. Y., & Taylor, D. M. (1977). Toward a Theory of Language in Ethnic Group Relations. In H. Giles (Ed.), *Language, Ethnicity and Intergroup Relations*. London: Academic Press.

Giles, H., Coupland, N., & Coupland, J. (1991). Accommodation Theory: Communication, Context, and Consequences. In H. Giles (Ed.), *Contexts of Accommodation: Development in Applied Sociolinguistics* (pp. 1 - 68). Cambridge: Cambridge University Press.

Giles, H., & Powesland, P. F. (1975). *Speech Style and Social Evaluation*. London: Academic Press.

Giles, H., & Smith, P. (1979). Accommodation Theory: Optimal Levels of Convergence. In H. Giles & R. St. Clair (Eds.), *Language and Society 1. Language and Social Psychology* (pp. 45 - 65). Baltimore: University Park Press.

Giles, H., Taylor, D. M., & Bourhis, R. Y. (1973). Toward a Theory of Interpersonal Accommodation Through Speech Accommodation: Some Canadian Data. *Language in Society, 2*, 177 - 192.

Giles, H., Taylor, D. M., Lambert, W. E., & Albert, G. (1976). Dimensions of Ethnic Identity: An Example From Northern Maine. *Journal of Social Psychology, 100*, 11 - 19.

Gilly, M. C. (1999). Unintended Effects of Advertsing. *Journal of Family and Consumer Sciences, 91*(3), 92.

Gitlin, S. (2001, Nov 19). Russian Addressing. *Brandweek, 42*, 19 - 20.

Goldberg, M. E., & Gorn, G. J. (1974). Children's Reactions To Television Advertising -- An Experimental Approach. *Journal Of Consumer Research, 1*(2), 69.

Goldberg, M. E., & Gorn, G. J. (1978). Some Unintended Consequences of TV Advertising to Children. *Journal of Consumer Research, 5*(1), 22.

Goldlust, J., & Richmond, A. H. (1977). Factors Associated with Commitment to and Identification with Canada. In W. W. Isajiw (Ed.), *Identities: The Impact of Ethnicity on Canadian Society* (pp. 132 - 153). Toronto: Peter Martin Associates.

Gooding, H. (1998, Jul 16). Racial Integration. *Marketing Week, 21*, 41 - 42.

Gordon, M. (1964). *Assimilation in American Life*. New York: Oxford University Press.

Grace, G. W. (1987). *The Linguistic Construction of Reality*. London: Routledge.

Greeley, A. M. (1971). *Why Can't They Be Like Us?* New York: E P Dutton.

Green, C. I. (1999). Ethnic Evaluations of Advertising: Interaction Effects of Strength of Ethnic Identification, Media Placement, and Degree of Racial Composition. *Journal of Advertising, 28*(1), 49 - 64.

Green, P. E., & Krieger, A. M. (1991). Segmenting Markets with Conjoint Analysis. *Journal of Marketing, 55*, 20 - 31.

Green, R. T., Cunningham, W. H., & Cunningham, I. C. M. (1978). The Effectiveness of Standard Global Advertising. *Journal of Advertising, 4*(3), 25 - 30.

Greenwald, A. G., & Banaji, M. R. (1995). Implicit Social Cognition: Attitudes, Self-Esteem, and Stereotypes. *Psychological Review, 102*(January), 4 - 27.

Grier, S. A., & Brumbaugh, A. M. (1999). Noticing Cultural Differences: Ad Meanings Created by Target and Non-target Markets. *Journal of Advertising, 28*(1), 79 - 93.

Grier, S. A., & Deshpande, R. (2001). Social Dimensions of Consumer Distinctiveness: The Influence of Social Status on Group Identity and Advertising Persuasion. *Journal of Marketing Research, 38*(2), 216 - 224.

Grossjean, F. (1982). *Life With Two Languages: An Introduction to Bilingualism.* Cambridge: Harvard University Press.

Gruber, A. (1970). Purchase Intent and Purchase Probability. *Journal of Advertising Research, 10*(1), 23 - 27.

Gulas, C. S., & McKeage, K. (2000). Extending Social Comparison: An Examination of the Unintended Consequences of Idealized Advertising Imagery. *Journal of Advertising, 29*(2), 17 - 28.

Gurak, D. T., & Fitzpatrick, J. P. (1982). Intermarriage Among Hispanic Ethnic Groups in New York city. *American Journal of Sociology, 87*(January), 921 - 934.

Hagendoorn, L. (1993). Ethnic Categorization and Outgroup Exclusion: Cultural Values and Social Stereotypes in the Construction of Ethnic Hierarchies. *Ethnic and Racial Studies, 16*(1), 26.

Hagendoorn, L. (1995). Intergroup Biases in Multiple Group Systems: The Perception of Ethnic Hierachies. *European Review of Social Psychology, 6*, 199 - 228.

Hair Jr., J. F., Anderson, R. E., Tatham, R. L., & Black, W. C. (1998). *Multivariate Data Analysis* (5 ed.). New Jersey: Prentice Hall International, Inc.

Hall, E. T. (1976). *Beyond Culture.* Garden City, NY: Anchor.

Hamilton, H. E. (1991). Accommodation and Mental Disability. In H. Giles (Ed.), *Contexts of Accommodation: Developments in Applied Sociolinguistics.* Cambridge: Cambridge University Press.

Hammond, K., Ehrenberg, A., & Goodhardt, G. J. (1995). *Market Segmentation for Competitive Brands* (Working Paper No. 95 - 201). London: London Business School.

Harris, G. (1994). International Advertising Standardization: What Do the Multinationals Actually Standardize? *Journal of International Marketing, 2*(4), 13 - 30.

Hecht, M. L., Collier, M. J., & Ribeau, S. A. (1993). *African American Communication: Ethnic Identity and Cultural Interpretation, Language and Languages Behavior* (Vol. 2). Newbury Park, CA: Sage.

Heider, F. (1958). *The Psychology of Interpersonal Relations.* New York.

Henthorne, T. L., LaTour, M. S., & Nataraajan, R. (1993). Fear Appeals in Print Advertising: An Analysis of Arousal and Ad Response. *Journal of Advertising, 22*(2), 59 - 69.

Herbig, P., & Milewicz, J. (1996). To Be or Not To Be.Credible That Is: A Model of Reputation and Credibility Among Competing Firms. *Corporate Communications, 1*(2), 19 - 30.

Herbig, P., & Yelkur, R. (1998). Marketing to Hispanics. *Journal of Professional Services Marketing, 16*(2), 171.

Hernandez, S. A., & Newman, L. M. (1992). Choice of English vs. Spanish Language in Advertising to Hispanics. *Journal of Current Issues and Research in Advertising, 14*(2), 35 -45.

Hewstone, M., Rubin, M., & Willis, H. (2002). Intergroup Bias. *Annual Review of Psychology, 53*, 575.

Hill, J. D. (1999, Nov 8). American Targets Black Market. *AdWeek, 20*, 6.

Hill, J. S., & Still, R. R. (1984). Effects of Urbanization on Multinational Product Planning: Markets in LCDs. *Columbia Journal of World Business, 19*(Summer), 62 - 67.

Hirschman, E. C. (1981). American Jewish Identity: Its Relationship to Some Selected Aspects of Consumer Behavior. *Journal of Marketing, 45*, 102 - 110.

Hirschman, E. C., & Thompson, C. J. (1997). Why Media Matter: Towards a Richer Understanding of Consumer's Relationship with Advertising and Mass Media. *Journal of Advertising, 26*(1), 43 - 60.

Ho, D. Y. (1972). On the Concept of Face. *American Journal of Sociology, 81*(4), 72 - 78.

Hodder, B. W. (1959). *Man in Malaysia*. London: University of London.

Hoek, J., Gendall, P., & Esslemont, D. H. B. (1996). Market Segmentation: A Search for the Holy Grail? *Journal of Marketing Practice: Applied Marketing Science, 2*(1), 25 - 34.

Hoffman, C. (1991). *An Introduction to Bilingualism*. New York: Longman.

Hofstede, G. (1991). *Cultures and Organizations - Software for the Mind*. London: McGraw-Hill.

Hogg, M., Abrams, D., & Patel, Y. (1987). Ethnic Identity, Self Esteem, and Occupational Aspirations of Indian and Anglo Saxon British Adolescents. *Genetics, Social, and General Psychology Monographs, 113*, 487 - 508.

Holbrook, M. B. (1986). Emotion in the Consumption Experience: Towards a New Model of the Human Consumer. In R. A. Peterson, W. D. Hoyer & W. R. Wilson (Eds.), *The Role of Affect in Consumer Behaviour: Emerging Theories and Applications*. Lexington, M.A.: D. C. Heath.

Holbrook, M. B., & Batra, R. (1987). Assessing the Role of Emotions as Mediators of Consumer Responses to Advertising. *Journal of Consumer Research, 14*(December), 404 - 419.

Holland, J., & Gentry, J. W. (1999). Ethnic Consumer Reaction to Targeted Marketing: A Theory of Intercultural Accommodation. *Journal of Advertising, 28*(1), 65.

Holmes, J. (1992). *An Introduction to Sociolinguistics*. London: Longman.

Homans, G. C. (1961). *Social Behavior: Its Elementary Forms*. New York: Harcourt, Brace, and World.

Hooley, G. J., Saunders, J. A., & Piercy, N. F. (1998). *Marketing Strategy and Competitive Positioning* (2 ed.): Prentice Hall.

Hraba, J. (1979). *American Ethnicity*. Ithaca: F.E. Peacock Publisher.

Hraba, J., Radloff, T., & Gray-Ray, P. (1999). A Comparison of Black and White Social Distance. *The Journal of Social Psychology, 139*(4), 536 - 539.

Hsu, F. L. K. (1983). *Rugged Individualism Reconsidered*. Knoxville: University of Tennessee Press.

Huhr, W. M., & Kim, K. C. (1984). Adhesive Sociocultural Adaptation of Korean Immigrants in the US: An Alternative Strategy of Minority Adaptation. *International Migration Review, 18*(2), 188 - 216.

Hui, M. K., Laroche, M., & Kim, C. (1998). A Typology of Consumption Based on Ethnic Origin and Media Usage. *European Journal of Marketing, 32*(9), 868 - 883.

Hunt, E., & Agnoli, F. (1991). The Whorfian Hypothesis: A Cognitive Psychology Perspective. *Psychological Review, 98*(3), 377 - 389.

Insko, C. A., Schopler, J., Hoyle, R., Dardis, G., & Graetz, K. (1990). Individual-group Discontinuity as a Function of Fear and Greed. *Journal of Personality and Social Psychology, 58*, 68 - 79.

Isajiw, W. W. (1980). Definitions of Ethnicity. In J. E. Goldstein & R. M. Bienvenue (Eds.), *Ethnic Relations in Canada: A Book of Readings* (pp. 13 - 25). Toronto: Butterworths.

Jabatan Perangkaan Malaysia. (1999). *Perangkaan Penting Malaysia.* Kuala Lumpur: Jabatan Perangkaan Malaysia.

Jabatan Perangkaan Malaysia Negeri Sarawak. (2002). *Siaran Perangkaan Bulanan Sarawak.* Kuching: Jabatan Percetakan Nasional Malaysia Berhad.

Jabatan Perangkaan Malaysia Negeri Sarawak. (2003). *Laporan Perangkaan Sarawak.* Kuching: Jabatan Percetakan Nasional Malaysia Berhad.

Jain, S. C. (1989). Standardization of International Marketing Strategy: Some Research Hypothesis. *Journal of Marketing, 63*(January), 70 - 79.

Jensen, P. C. (1998). *An Empirical Study of the Distinctiveness Theory as it Applies to Advertising Effectiveness.* Lamar University, Beaumont.

Johnson, M. K., & Sherman, S. J. (1990). Constructing and Reconstructing the Past and the Future in the Present. In E. T. Higgins & R. M. Sorentino (Eds.), *Handbook of Motivation and Cognition: Foundation of Social Behavior* (Vol. 2). New York: The Guilford Press.

Jones, E. E., & Davis, K. E. (1965). From Acts to Dispositions: The Attribution Process in Perception. In L. Berkowitz (Ed.), *Advances in Social Psychology* (Vol. 11). New York & London: Academic Press.

Joseph, T., & Holden, M. (2001). The Malaysian Dilemma: Advertising's Catalytic and Cataclysmic Role in Social Development. *Media, Culture, and Society, 23*, 275 - 297.

Juster, F. T. (1966). *Consumer Buying Intentions and Purchase Probability* (Occasional Paper 99): National Bureau of Economic Research, Colombia University Press.

Kale, S. H., & Sudharshan, D. (1987). Strategic Approach to International Segmentation. *International Marketing Review, 4*(Summer), 60 - 71.

Kasheira, Y. L., & Smith, M. E. (1943). A study of the Attitudes of Some Children of Japanese Descent Towards the Chinese and Japanese. *Journal of Social Psychology, 18*, 149 - 153.

Kates, S. M. (1997). *Closets are for Clothes: Understanding Gay Men's Consumer Behavior*: Haworth DDC.

Kates, S. M. (1999). Making the Ad Perfectly Queer: Marketing "Normality" to the Gay Men's Community? *Journal of Advertising, 28*(1), 25 - 37.

Kates, S. M. (2000). Out of the Closet and Out on the Street! Gay Men and Their Brand Relationship. *Psychology and Marketing, 17*(6), 493 - 513.

Kates, S. M., & Belk, R. W. (2001). The Meanings of Lesbian and Gay Pride Day: Resistance Through Consumption and Resistance to Consumption. *Journal of Contemporary Ethnography, 30*(4), 392 - 429.

Katz, D., & Braly, K. (1933). Racial Stereotypes of One Hundred College Students. *Journal of Abnormal and Social Psychology, 28*, 280 - 290.

Keefe, S. E., & Padilla, A. M. (1987). *Chicano Ethnicity.* Albuquerque, NM: University of New Mexico Press.

Keegan, W. J., Still, R. R., & Hill, J. S. (1987). Transferability and Adapatibility of Products and Promotion Themes in Multinational Marketing-MNCs in LCDs. *Journal of Global Marketing, 1*(Fall / Winter), 86 - 103.

Kelly, G. A. (1955). *The Psychology of Personal Constructs*. New York: Norton.

Kelly, H. H. (1973). The Process of Causal Attribution. *American Psychologist, 28*, 107 - 128.

Kennedy, R., & Ehrenberg, A. (2001). There is No Segmentation. *Marketing Insights*(Spring), 4 - 7.

Keyes, C. F. (1976). Towards a New Formulation of the Concept of Ethnic Group. *Ethnicity, 2*, 202 - 213.

Kim, Y. K., & Kang, J. (2001). The Effects of Ethnicity and Product on Purchase Decision Making. *Journal of Advertising Research, 41*(2), 39 - 48.

Kim, Y. Y. (1977). Communication Patterns of Foreign Immigrants in the Process of Acculturation. *Human Communication Research, 4*, 66 - 77.

Kim, Y. Y. (1978). A Communication Approach to Acculturation Processes: Korean Immigrants in Chicago. *International Journal of Intercultural Relations, 2*(2), 197 - 224.

King, E. (1991). Cover Story: Habla Espanol? *Target Marketing, 14*(10), 10.

Kinra, N. (1997). The Communicative Effectiveness of Ethnically Oriented Advertising. *International Journal of Advertising, 16*(3), 221 - 239.

Kitano, H. H. L. (1985). *Race Relations*. Englewood Cliffs, NJ: Prentice Hall.

Klegg, M., & Yamamoto, K. (1998). As the World Turns: Ethno-racial Distances After 70 Years. *The Social Science Journal, 35*(2), 183 - 190.

Kluckhohn, R. (1962). *Culture and Behavior: Collected Essays of Clyde Kluckhohn*. New York: The Free Press of Glencoe / MacMillan.

Koslow, S., Shamdasani, P. N., & Touchstone, E. E. (1994). Exploring Language Effects in Ethnic Advertising: A Sociolinguistic Perspective. *Journal of Consumer Research, 20*, 575 - 585.

Kotler, P. (1986). Global Markets or Global Competition? *Journal of Consumer Marketing, 3*(Spring), 13 - 15.

Kotler, P. (1997). *Marketing Management: Analysis, Planing, Implementation, and Control* (9 ed.). Englewood Cliffs, NJ: Prentice Hall.

Kotler, P., & Armstrong, G. (1994). *Principles of Marketing* (6 ed.). Englewood Cliffs, NJ: Prentice Hall.

Kotler, P., Swee, H. A., Siew, M. L., & Chin, T. A. (1999). *Marketing Management Asian Perspective*: Prentice Hall.

Krackhardt, D., & Kilduff, M. (1999). Whether Close or Far: Social Distance Effects on Perceived Balance in Friendship Networks. *Journal of Personality and Social Psychology, 76*(5), 770 - 782.

Kruglanski, A. W. (1990). Motivations for Judging and Knowing: Implications for Causal Attribution. In E. T. Higgins & R. M. Sorentino (Eds.), *Handbook of Motivation and Cognition: Foundation of Social Behavior* (Vol. 2). New York: The Guilford Press.

Kumar, S. R. (2002, Oct 24). The Ethnic Way of Communication:Whatever the Product, Leveraging Ethnicity to Create Advertisements That the Market Can Easily Identify With Will Go a Long Way. *Businessline*, 1.

Kunz, J., & Kunz, P. R. (2001). Social Distance of Deviants and Deviant Offenders. *Psychological Reports, 88*(2), 505 - 513.

Kunz, P. R., & Oheneba-Sakyi, Y. (1989). Social Distance: A Study of Changing Views of Young Mormons Toward Black Individuals. *Psychological Reports, 65*(1), 195 - 200.

Lambert, W. E., & Taylor, D. M. (1990). *Coping with Cultural and Racial Diversity in Urban America*. New York: Praeger.

Lang, G. E., & Lang, K. (1986). Some Observations on the Long Range Effects of Television. In S. Ball-Rokeach & M. G. Cantor (Eds.), *Media, Audience, and Social Structure*. Newbury Park: Sage.

Laroche, M., Joy, A., Hui, M., & Kim, C. (1992). An Examination of Ethnicity Measures: Convergent Validity and Cross-cultural Equivalence. *Advances in Consumer Research, 18*, 150 - 157.

Laroche, M., Kim, C., & Tomiuk, M. A. (1999). Italian Ethnic Identity and its Relative Impact on the Consumption of Convenience and Traditional Foods. *British Food Journal, 101*(3), 201 - 228.

Laroche, M., Kirpalani, V. H., & Darmon, R. (1999). Determinants of the Control of International Advertising by Headquarters of Multinational Corporations. *Revue Canadienne Des Sciences de l'Administration, 16*(4), 273 - 290.

Lawrence, C., Shapiro, S. J., & Lalji, S. (1986). Ethnic Markets - A Canadian Perspective. *Academy of Marketing Science, 14*(2), 7.

Lazarfeld, P. F., Berelson, B., & Gaudet, H. (1944). *The People's Choice*. New York: Duell, Sloan, and Pearce.

Lee, K. H., & Tan, C. B. (2000). *The Chinese In Malaysia*. New York: Oxford University Press.

Lee, M. Y., Sapp, S. G., & Ray, M. C. (1996). The Reverse Social Distance Scale. *The Journal of Social Psychology, 136*(1), 17.

Lee, W. (1993). Acculturation and Advertising Communication Strategies: A Cross-cultural Study of Chinese and Americans. *Psychology & Marketing, 10*(5), 381 - 397.

Lee, W., & Tse, D. K. (1994a). Becoming Canadian: Understanding How Hong Kong Immigrants Change Their Consumption. *Pacific Affairs, 67*(1), 70 - 95.

Lee, W., & Tse, D. K. (1994b). Changing Media Consumption in a New Home: Acculturation Patterns among Hong Kong Immigrants to Canada. *Journal of Advertising, 23*(1), 57 - 70.

Lenormand, J. M. (1964). East Europe Ripe for the Integration of Advertising? *The International Advertiser, 5*(3), 12 - 14.

Lindridge, A., & Dibb, S. (2003). Is 'Culture' a Justifiable Variable for Market Segmentation? A Cross-cultural Example. *Journal of Consumer Behavior, 2*(3), 269 - 286.

Linell, P. (1991). Accommodation on Trial: Processes of Communicative Accommodation in Courtroom Interaction. In H. Giles (Ed.), *Contexts of Accommodation: Developments in Applied Sociolinguistics*. Cambridge: Cambridge University Press.

Link, B. G., Phelan, J. C., Bresnahan, M., Stueve, A., & Pescosolido, B. A. (1999). Public Conceptions of Mental Illness: Labels, Causes, Dangerousness, and Social Distance. *American Journal of Public Health, 89*(9), 1328 - 1333.

Lipski, J. M. (1985). Spanish in United States Broadcasting. In L. Elisas-Olivares (Ed.), *Spanish Language Use and Public Life in the United States* (pp. 217 - 233). Berlin: Mouton.

Livingston, S. (1992). Marketing to Hispanic- American Community. *Journal of Business Strategy, 13*(2), 54 - 57.

Low, H. (1848). *Sarawak: Its inhabitants and productions*. London: Richard Bentley.

Luna, D., & Peracchio, L. A. (2001). Moderators of Language Effects in Advertising to Bilinguals: A Psycholinguistic Approach. *Journal of Consumer Research, 28*(2), 284.

Luna, D., & Peracchio, L. A. (2002). Uncovering the Cognitive Duality of Bilinguals Through Word Association. *Psychology & Marketing, 19*(6), 457.

Lyman, S. M. (1995). Interstate Relations and the Sociological Imagination Revisited: From Social Distance to Territoriality. *Sociological Inquiry, 65*, 125 - 142.

Mackie, D. M., & Smith, E. R. (1998). Intergroup relations: Insights from a theoretically integrative approach. *Psychological Review, 105*, 499 - 529.

Macnamara, J. (1969). How can one measure the extent of a person's bilingual proficiency? In K. L. G. (Ed.), *Description and Measurement of bilingualism: An international seminar* (Vol. 79 - 97). Toronto.

Macrae, N. C., & Bodenhausen, G. V. (2000). Social Cognition: Thinking Categorically about Others. *Annual Review of Psychology, 51*, 93 - 120.

Madden, C. S., Easley, R. W., & Dunn, M. G. (1995). How journal editors view replication research. *Journal of Advertising, 24*(4), 77 - 88.

Maheswaran, D., & Sternthal, B. (1990). The effects of knowledge, motivation, and type of message on ad processing and product judgements. *Journal of Consumer Research, 17*(June), 66 - 73.

Mainous, A. G. (1989). Self-concept as an indicator of acculturation in Mexican-Americans. *Hispanic Journal of Behavioral Sciences, 11*(2), 178 - 189.

Makabe, T. (1979). Ethnic identity scale and social mobility: The case of Nisei in Toronto. *The Canadian Review of Sociology and Anthropology, 16*, 136 - 145.

Malat, J. (2001). Social distance and patients' rating of healthcare providers. *Journal of Health and Social Behavior, 42*(4), 360.

Mardiana, H. (2000). *Pengajian Malaysia*. Kuala Lumpur: Penerbit Fajar Bakti Sdn Bhd.

Marin, G., Sabogal, F., Van Oss-Marin, B., Otero-Sabogal, R., & Perez-Stable, E. J. (1987). Developments of a short acculturation scale for Hispanics. *Hispanic Journal of Behavioral Sciences, 9*(2), 183 - 205.

Marshall, E. (1998). DNA studies challenge the meaning of race. *Science, 282*(5389), 654 - 655.

Martin, M. C., & Gentry, J. W. (1997). Stuck in the model trap: The effects of beautiful models in Ads on female pre-adolescents and adolescents. *Journal of Advertising, 26*(2), 19 - 33.

Martin, M. C., & Kennedy, P. F. (1993). Advertising and social comparison: Consequences for female preadolescent and adolescent. *Psychology and Marketing, 10*(6), 513 - 530.

Massey, D. S., & Mulan, B. P. (1984). Processes of Hispanic and Black spatial assimilation. *American Journal of Sociology, 89*(January), 836 - 873.

Masuda, M., Matsumoto, G. H., & Meredith, G. M. (1970). Ethnic identity in three generations of Japanese Americans. *The Journal of Social Psychology, 81*, 199 - 207.

McAlister, F. A., Straus, S. E., Sackett, D. L., & Altman, D. G. (2003). Analysis and reporting of Factorial trials: A Systematic Review. *Journal of the American Medical Association, 289*(19), 2545 - 2553.

McCombs, M. E., & Shaw, D. L. (1972). The agenda-setting function of the media. *Public Opinion Quarterly, 36*, 176 - 187.

McFee, M. (1968). The 150% man: a product of Blackfeet acculturation. *American Anthropologist, 70*, 1096 - 1103.

McGuire, W. (1984). Search for the Self: Going beyond self-esteem and the reactive self. In R. A. Zucker, J. Aronoff & A. T. Rabin (Eds.), *Personality and the prediction of behavior* (pp. 73 - 120). New York: Academic Press.

McGuire, W., & McGuire, C., V. (1979). Effects of household sex composition on the salience of one's gender in the spontaneous self-concept. *Journal of Experimental Social Psychology, 15*(1), 77 - 90.

McGuire, W., & McGuire, C., V. (1981). The spontaneous self-concept as affected by personal distinctiveness. In M. D. Lynch & K. Gergen (Eds.), *Self-concept: Advances in Theory and Research* (pp. 147 - 171). New York: Ballinger.

McKelvie, S. J., & MacGregor, R. M. (1996). Effects of interactive pictures and ethnicity on recall of brand names. *Revue Canadienne des Sciences de l'Administration, 13*(1), 33.

McKenna, S. (1992). *The complete guide to regional marketing.* Homewood: Business One Irwin.

McQuail, D. (1983). *Mass communication theory: An introduction.* London: Sage Productions.

McQuail, D., & Windahl, S. (1993). *Communication models: For the study of mass communication* (2 ed.). New York: Longman.

McQuarrie, E. F., & Mick, D. G. (1992). On resonance: a critical pluralistic inquiry into advertising rhetoric. *Journal of Consumer Research, 19*(September), 180 - 197.

McQuarrie, E. F., & Mick, D. G. (1999). Visual rhetoric in advertising: Text-interpretive, experimental, and reader-response analyses. *Journal of Consumer Research, 26*(1), 37 - 54.

Mehra, A., Kilduff, M., & Brass, D. J. (1998). At the margins: A Distinctiveness approach to the social identity and social networks of underrepresented groups. *Academy of Management Journal, 41*(4), 441.

Mehrotra, S. (1990). Strategic regional marketing: Two plus two equals six. *Journal of Advertising Research, 30*(December / January), 9 - 17.

Mendoza, R. H. (1989). An empirical scale to measure type and degree of acculturation in Mexican-American adolescents and adults. *Journal of Cross-Cultural Psychology, 20*(4), 372 - 385.

Mick, D., & Buhl, C. (1992). A meaning-based model of advertising experiences. *Journal of Consumer Research, 19*(December), 317 - 338.

Mick, D., & Politi, L. G. (1989). Consumers' interpretations of advertising imagery. A visit to the hell of connotation. In E. C. Hirschman (Ed.), *Interpretive Cnsumer Research* (pp. 85 - 96). Provo: Association for Consumer Research.

Milne, R. S. (1978). *Government and Politics in Malaysia.* Boston: Houghton Mifflin Company.

Mirowsky, J., & Ross, C. E. (1980). Minority status, ethnic culture, and distress: A comparison of blacks, whites, Mexicans, and Mexican-American. *American Journal of Sociology, 86*(November), 479 - 495.

Mitchel, A. A. (1986). The effect of verbal and visual components of advertisements on brand attitudes and attitude towards the advertisement. *Journal of Consumer Research, 13*(1), 12 - 14.

Mitchell, A. A., & Olson, J. C. (1981). Are Product Attribute Beliefs The Only Mediator Of Advertising Effects On Brand Attitude? *Journal Of Marketing Research, 18*, 318 - 322.

106

Mitchell, V. W. (1995). Using astrology in market segmentation. *Management Decision, 33*(1), 48 - 57.

Mittal, B. (1995). A comparative analysis of four scales of consumer involvement. *Psychology & Marketing, 12*(7), 663 - 682.

Mohl, B. (2002). Customers want their prize for loyalty. *Boston Globe,* p. C3.

Montgomery, M. (1988). DJ Talk. In N. Coupland (Ed.), *Styles of Discourse* (pp. 85 - 104). London: Croom Helm.

Morais, F. (1996). *Understanding Advertising.* Kuala Lumpur: Berita Publishing Sdn. Bhd.

Morris, C. (1946). *Signs, Language and Behavior.* Englewood Cliffs, NJ: Prentice Hall.

Moscovisi, S. (1975). *Social Influence and Social Change.* London: Academic Press.

Mueller, B. (1992). Standardization vs. Specialization: An Examination of Westernization in Japanese Advertising. *Journal of Advertising Research, 32*(1), 15 - 24.

Mulac, A., Wiemann, J. M., Widenmann, S. J., & Gibson, T. W. (1988). Male/female language differences and effects in same sex and mixed sex dyads: the gender linked language effect. *Communication Monographs, 55*, 315 - 335.

Mummert, H. (1995). Reaching Ethnic Markets. *Zip/Target Marketing, 18*(11), 14 - 16.

Murphy, R., & Crowther, D. (2002). Social responsibility and marketing: An agenda for research. *Management Decision, 40*(4), 302 - 310.

Myers, P. N., & Biocca, F. A. (1992). The elastic body image: The effect of television advertising and programming on body image distortion in young women. *Journal of Communication, 42*(Summer), 108 - 133.

Nazaruddin, H. M. J., Ma'rof, R., Asnarulkhadi, A. S., & Ismail, H. M. R. (2001). *Pengajian Malaysia, Kenegaraan, Dan Kewarganegaraan.* Kuala Lumpur: Prentice Hall.

Nelson Jr., J. R., & Lukas, J. E. (1990). Target: Minorities. *Marketing & Media Decisions, 25*(10), 70 - 72.

Newell, S. J., & Goldsmith, R. E. (2001). The development of a scale to measure perceived corporate credibility. *Journal of Business Research, 52*, 235 - 247.

Nicholls, J. A. F., & Roslow, P. (1999). Effectiveness of Spanish versus English language TV commercials targeted to the Hispanic market. *Journal of Promotion Management, 5*(1), 57 - 75.

Noriah, M. (1994). Waktu pisah dan tingkat kekerabatan Bahasa Melayu dan Bahasa Iban. *Jurnal Dewan Bahasa*(Feb.), 129 - 143.

Nunnally, J. C., & Bernstein, I. H. (1994). *Psychometric Theory* (3 ed.). New York: McGraw-Hill, Inc.

O'Guinn, T. C., Allen, C. T., & Semenik, R. J. (2003). *Advertising and Integrated Brand Promotion* (3 ed.). USA: South Western.

O'Guinn, T. C., Faber, R. J., & Meyer, T. P. (1985). Ethnic segmentation and Spanish-language television. *Journal of Advertising, 14*(3), 63.

Oakes, P. J. (1987). The Salience of Social Categories. In J. C. Turner (Ed.), *Rediscovering the Social Group: A Self-Categorization Theory* (pp. 117 - 141). New York: Basil Blackwell.

Ober, S. (1995). *Contemporary business communication* (2 ed.). Boston: Houghton Mifflin Company.

Olmedo, E. L. (1979). Acculturation: a psychometric perspective. *American Psychologist, 34*, 1061 - 1070.

Ottesen, O. (1981). Long run effects of advertising: A conceptual discussion. *European Research, 9*(2), 46 - 59.

Paivio, A. (1971). *Imagery and verbal processes*. New York: Holt, Rinehart & Winston.

Pavlik, J. V. (1987). *Public Relations: What research tells us*. Newbury Park: Sage.

Payne Jr., M. C., York, C. M., & Fagan, J. (1974). Changes in measured social distance over time. *Sociometry, 37*, 131 - 136.

Penaloza, L. (1994). Atravesando Fronteras / Border crossings: A critical ethnographic exploration of the consumer acculturation of Mexican immigrants. *Journal of Consumer Research, 21*(June), 32 - 54.

Petersen, L. M. (1992, Nov 30). Advertisers look to Asian immigrants. *Mediaweek, 2*, 2.

Peterson, R. A., Wilson, W. R., & Brown, S. P. (1992). Effects of advertised customer satisfaction claims on consumer attitudes and purchase intention. *Journal of Advertising Research, 32*(2), 34 - 40.

Peterson, R. T. (1987). Bullimia and Anorexia in an advertising context. *Journal of Business Ethics, 6*, 495 - 504.

Petty, R. E., & Cacioppo, J. T. (1981). *Attitudes and Persuasion: Classic and Contemporary Approaches*. Dubuque, IA: Brown.

Phinney, J. S. (1990). Ethnic identity in adolescent and adults: Review of research. *Psychological Bulletin, 108*(3), 499 - 514.

Piatila, V. (1977). On the effects of mass media: Some conceptual viewpoints. In M. Berg, P. Hemanus, J. Ekecrantz, F. Mortensen & P. Sepstrup (Eds.), *Current Theories in Scandinavian Mass Communication Research*. Grenaa: GMT.

Pickering, J. F., & Isherwood, B. C. (1974). Purchase Probabilities and Consumer Durable Buying Behaviour. *Journal of the Market Research Society, 16*(3), 203 - 226.

Pierce, R. C., Clark, M. M., & Kaufman, S. (1978). Generation and ethnic identity: A typological analysis. *International Journal of Aging and Human Development, 9*(1), 19 - 29.

Pingjun, J. (2000). Segment-based mass customization: an exploration of a new conceptual marketing framework. *Internet Research, 10*(3), 215 - 226.

Pinson, L., & Jinnett, J. (1993). *Target marketing for the small business*: Upstart Publishing Co.

Platt, J. (1981). The Chinese community in Malaysia: Language policies and relationships. In J. Megarry, S. Nisbet & E. Hoyle (Eds.), *World Yearbook of Education 1981: Education of Minorities*. London: Kogan Page.

Platt, J., & Weber, H. (1984). Speech convergence miscarried: An investigation into inappropriate accommodation strategies. *International Journal of the Sociology of Language, 46*, 131 - 146.

Pollak, K. I., & Niemann, Y. F. (1998). Black and white tokens in academia: a difference of chronic versus acute distinctiveness. *Journal of Applied Social Psychology [H.W. Wilson - SSA], 28*(11), 954.

Pollay, R. W. (1986). The distorted mirror: Reflections on the unintended consequences of advertising. *Journal of Marketing, 50*(April), 18 - 36.

Pollay, R. W., & Gallagher, K. (1990). Advertising and cultural values: Reflections in the distorted mirror. *International Journal of Advertising, 9*(4), 359 - 372.

Pollay, R. W., Lee, J. S., & Carter-Whitney, D. (1992). Separate, but not equal: racial segmentation in cigarette advertising. *Journal of Advertising, 21*(1), 45 - 58.

Pornpitakpan, C. (1999). The effects of cultural adaptation on business relationships: Americans selling to Japanese and Thais. *Journal of International Business Studies, 30*(2 (Second Quarter)), 317 - 338.

Pornpitakpan, C. (2003). Cultural adaptation and business relationships: Americans selling to Indonesians, Malaysians, and People's Republic of China Chinese. *Journal of Global Marketing, 16*(3), 75.

Porter, E. (2002, Apr 19). Hispanic-targeted advertising outpaces overall ad growth. *Wall Street Journal*, p. A.17.

Postill, J. (1999). The Impact of Television and Radio on the rural Iban of Sarawak, East Malaysia: An ethnographic report. *Sarawak Development Journal, 2*(2), 91 - 109.

Prabu, D., Morrison, G., Johnson, M. A., & Ross, F. (2002). Body image, race, and fashion models: Social distance and social identification in third-person effects. *Communication Research, 29*(3), 270 - 294.

Preston, C. (1999). The unintended effects of advertising upon children. *International Journal of Advertising, 18*(3), 363 - 377.

Pringle, R. (1970). *Rajahs and Rebels: The Iban of Sarawak under Brooke Rule, 1841 - 1941*. Ithaca: Cornell University Press.

Prothrow-Stith, D., & Spivak, H. (1998, Jul 26). The wrong images for kids. *Boston Globe*, p. D7.

Purcell, V. (1965). *Malaysia*. London: Thames and Hudson Ltd.

Quinn, N. (1992). The Motivational Force of Self-Understanding: Evidence from Wives' Inner Conflict. In R. G. D'Andrade & C. Strauss (Eds.), *Human Motives and Cultural Models* (pp. 90 - 126). Cambridge: Cambridge University Press.

Quinn, N., & Holland, D. (1987). Culture and Cognition. In D. Holland & N. Quinn (Eds.), *Cultural Models in Language and Thought* (pp. 222 - 242). Cambridge: Cambridge University Press.

Raden, D. (1998). American Blacks' and Whites' preferred social distance from Jews. *The Journal of Social Psychology, 138*(2), 265 - 267.

Ramsay, J. O. (1973). The Effect of Number of Categories in Rating Scales on Precision of Estimation of Scale Values. *Psychometrica, 38*(4), 513 - 532.

Reilly, M. D., & Wallendorf, M. (1984). A longitudinal study of Mexican-American assimilation. In T. Kinnear (Ed.), *Advances in Consumer Research* (Vol. 11, pp. 735 - 740). Provo, UT: Association for Consumer Research.

Remmers, H. H. (1934). Studies in Attitudes - A contribution to social psychological methods. *Studies in Higher Education - Bulletin Purdue University, 26*, 112.

Renzetti, C. M., & Curran, D. J. (1998). *Living Sociology*: Allyn and Bacon.

Resnick, L. B. (1991). Shared Cognition: Thinking as Social Practice. In L. Resnick, J. M. Levine & S. D. Teasley (Eds.), *Perspectives on Socially Shared Cognition* (pp. 1 - 20). Washington, DC: American Psychological Association.

Richins, M. L. (1991). Social comparison and the idealized images of advertising. *Journal of Consumer Research, 18*(June), 71 - 83.

Richins, M. L. (1996). Materialism, desire, and discontent. In R. P. Hill (Ed.), *Marketing and Consumer Research in the Public Interest* (Vol. 109 - 132). CA: Sage.

Ringold, D. J. (1995). Social criticism of target marketing: process or product? (Social advocacy: Marketing and consumer behavior research in the public interest). *American Behavioral Scientist, 38*(4), 578 - 593.

Robinson, J. (1938). *The economics of imperfect competition*. London: Macmillan.

Rogler, L. H., Cortes, D. E., & Malgady, R. G. (1991). Acculturation and mental health among Hispanics: convergence and new direction for research. *American Psychologist, 46*(6), 585 - 597.

Rosenthal, D. A., & Feldman, S. S. (1992). The nature and stability of ethnic identity in Chinese youths: Effects of length of residence in two cultural contexts. *Journal of Cross-cultural Psychology, 23*(2), 214 - 227.

Rosenthal, R., & Rosnow, R. L. (1991). *Essentials of Behavioral Research. Methods and Data Analysis* (2 ed.). Boston: McGraw Hill.

Roslow, P., & Nicholls, J. A. F. (1996). Targeting the Hispanic market: Comparative persuasion of TV commercials in Spanish and English. *Journal of Advertising Research, 36*(3), 67.

Rotfled, H. (1999, Feb 15). Your flaming arrow might hit wrong target. *Marketing News, 33*, 6, 8.

Roth, H. L. (1896). *The native of Sarawak and British North Borneo*. London: Truslove and Hanson.

Roth, M. S. (1995). Effects of global market conditions on brand image customization and brand performance. *Journal of Advertising, 24*(4), 55.

Roth, M. S., & Moorman, C. (1988). The Cultural Content of Cognition and the Cognitive Content of Culture: Implications for Consumer Research. In M. Houston (Ed.), *Advances in Consumer Research* (Vol. 15, pp. 403 - 410). Provo, UT: Association for Consumer Research.

Rusbult, C., Verette, J., Whitney, G., Slovik, L., & Lipkus, I. (1991). Accommodation Processes in Close Relationships. *Journal of Personality and Social Psychology, 60*, 53 - 78.

Ryan, M. J., & Bonfield, E. H. (1975). The Fishbein Extended Model and Consumer Behaviour. *Journal of Consumer Research, 2*(September), 118 - 136.

Saegert, J., Hoover, R. J., & Hilger, M. T. (1985). Characteristics of Mexican-American consumers. *Journal of Consumer Research, 12*, 104 - 109.

Samiee, S., & Roth, K. (1992). The influence of global marketing standardization on performance. *Journal of Marketing, 66*(April), 1 - 17.

Santoro, E. (1991, October). Hispanics are hot. *Direct Marketing, 54*, 28 - 32.

Schermerhorn, R. A. (1970). *Comparative ethnic relations: A framework for theory and research*. New York: RandomHouse.

Schiffman, L., & Kanuk, L. (1997). *Consumer Behaviour* (6 ed.). USA: Prentice Hall.

Schmitt, B. H., Pan, Y., & Tavassoli, N. T. (1994). Language and consumer memory: The impact of linguistic differences between Chinese and English. *Journal of Consumer Research, 21*(December), 419 - 431.

Schmitt, B. H., Tavassoli, N. T., & Millard, R. T. (1993). Memory for print ads: Understanding relations among brand name, copy, and picture. *Journal of Consumer Psychology, 2*(1), 55 - 81.

Schram, P. J. (1999). Social distance between inmates, peer counselors, and program staff in a woman's prison. *Journal of Offender Rehabilitation, 29*(1-2), 89 - 100.

Schudson, M. (1994). Culture and the integration of national societies. *International Social Science Journal, 46*, 63.

Schwartz, S., & Link, B. G. (1991). Separating Class and Ethnic Prejudice: A Study of North African and European Jews in Israel. *Social Psychology Quarterly, 54*(4), 287.

Scott, L. M. (1990). Understanding jingles and needledrop: A rhetorical approach to music in advertising. *Journal of Consumer Research, 17*(September), 223 - 237.

Scott, L. M. (1994a). The bridge from text to mind: Adapting reader-response theory to consumer research. *Journal of Consumer Research, 21*(December), 461 - 481.

Scott, L. M. (1994b). Images in advertising: The need for a theory of visual rhetoric. *Journal of Consumer Research, 21*(September), 252 - 273.

Segal, M., & Sosa, L. (1983). Marketing to the Hispanic community. *California Management Review, 26*(6), 120 - 134.

Seitz, V. (1998). Acculturation and direct purchasing behavior among ethnic groups in the US: implications for business practitioners. *The Journal of Consumer Marketing, 15*(1), 23 - 31.

Servaes, J. (1989). Cultural identity and modes of communication. In J. A. Anderson (Ed.), *Communication Yearbook* (Vol. 12, pp. 383 - 417). Newbury Park: Sage Publications.

Shaffer, T. R., & O'Hara, B. S. (1995). The effects of country of origin on trust and ethical perceptions of legal services. *Service Industries Journal, 15*(2), 162 - 185.

Shanklin, E. (1993). *Anthropology and Race*. Belmont, CA: Wadsworth.

Shepard, R. N. (1967). Recognition memory for words, sentences, and pictures. *Journal of Verbal Learning and Verbal Behavior, 6*(February), 156 - 163.

Shoham, A. (1996). Effectiveness of standardize and adapted television advertising: An international field study approach. *Journal of International Consumer Marketing, 9*(1), 5 - 23.

Sidanius, J., & Pratto, F. (1999). *Social Dominance: An Intergroup Theory of Social Hierachy and Oppression*. New York: Cambridge University Press.

Silverstein, B., Perdue, L., Peterson, B., & Kelly, E. (1986). The role of the mass media in promoting a thin standard of bodily attractiveness for women. *Sex Roles, 14*(9 - 10), 519 - 532.

Simard, L., Taylor, D. M., & Giles, H. (1976). Attribution processes and interpersonal accommodation in a bilingual setting. *Language and Speech, 19*, 374 - 387.

Simpson, E. M., Snuggs, T., Christiansen, T., & Simples, K. E. (2000). Race, homophily, and purchase intentions and the black consumer. *Psychology & Marketing, 17*(10), 877 - 889.

Smith, B. M., Bruner, J. S., & White, R. W. (1956). *Opinions and Personality*. New York: Wiley.

Smith, E. J. (1989). Black Racial Identity Development: Issues and Concerns. *The Counseling Psychologist, 17*, 277 - 288.

Smith, E. J. (1991). Ethnic Identity Development: Toward the Development of a Theory Within the Context of Majority/Minority Status. *Journal of Counseling and Development, 70*((September/October)), 181 -188.

Smith, E. R. (1993). Social identity and social emotions: Towards new conceptualizations. In D. Mackie & D. Hamilton (Eds.), *Affect, Cognition, and Stereotyping* (pp. 297 - 315). San Diego, CA: Academic.

Smith, E. R., & Henry, S. (1996). An in-group becomes part of the self: response, evidence. *Personality and Social Psychology Bulletin, 25*, 635 - 642.

Smith, R. G. (1970). *Speech-communication: Theory and Models*. New York: Harper and Row.

Smith, W. R. (1956). Product differentiation and market segmentation as alternative marketing strategies. *Journal of Marketing Research*, 3 - 8.

Solomon, M. R. (1999). *Consumer Behavior. Buying, Having, and Being*. New Jersey: Prentice Hall.

Somasundaram, T. N., & Light, D. C. (1994). Rethinking a global media strategy: A four country comparison of young adults' perceptions of media-specific advertising. *Journal of International Consumer Marketing, 7*(1), 23 - 38.

Spencer, B. C. (1999). *An examination of the relationship between corporate image and sponsorship*. Unpublished Master of Business, University of Otago, Dunedin.

Starch, D. (1966). How does the shape of ads affect readership? *Media/Scope, 10*, 83 - 85.

Steere, J. (1995, Mar 13). How Asian-Americans Make Purchase Decisions. *Marketing News, 29*, 9.

Steiner, G. (1975). *After Babel: Aspects of Language and Translations*. London: Oxford University Press.

Stephan, W. G., & Stephan, C. W. (2000). An integrated threat theory of prejudice. In S. Oskamp (Ed.), *Reducing Prejudice and Discrimination* (pp. 23 - 46). Mahwah, NJ: Erlbaum.

Stern, B. (1990). Other-speak: Classical allegory and contemporary advertising. *Journal of Advertising, 19*(3), 14 - 26.

Steward, D. W. (1994). Advertising in a slow-growth economy. *American Demographics, 16*(9), 40 - 47.

Street Jr., R. L. (1991). Accommodation in medical consultations. In H. Giles (Ed.), *Contexts of Accommodation: Developments in Applied Sociolinguistics*. Cambridge: University Press.

Suchan, J., & Dulek, R. (1988). Toward a better understanding of reader analysis. *The Journal of Business Communication, 25*(2), 29 - 45.

Suzuki, S. (1998). In-group and out-group communication patterns in international organizations. *Communication Research, 25*(2), 154 - 182.

Swift, J. S. (1991). Foreign language ability and international marketing. *European Journal of Marketing, 25*(12), 36 - 49.

Szapocznik, J., Kurtines, W., & Fernandez, T. (1980). Bicultural involvement and adjustment of Hispanic American youths. *International Journal of Intercultural Relations, 4*, 353 - 365.

Szymanski, D. M., Bharadwaj, S. G., & Varadarajan, P. R. (1993). Standardization vs. adaptation of international marketing strategy: An empirical investigation. *Journal of Marketing, 57*(October), 1 - 17.

Tajfel, H. (1974). Social identity and intergroup behaviour. *Social Science Information, 13*, 65 - 93.

Tajfel, H. (1981). *Human Groups and Social Categories*. Cambridge, UK: Cambridge University Press.

Tan, C. T., & Farley, J. U. (1987). The impact of cultural patterns on cognition and intention in Singapore. *Journal of Consumer Research, 13*(4), 540 - 545.

Tawai, J. (1997, 1 - 2 November). *Masalah dan masa depan yang dihadapi didalam pendidikan Bahasa ibunda bagi Bahasa Iban di Malaysia: Suatu laporan ringkas*. Paper presented at the Seminar on Mother Tongue Education of Malaysian Ethnic Mnorities, Dong Jiao Zong Campus, Kajang, Malaysia.

Teske, R. H. C., & Nelson, B. H. (1973). Two scale of measurements of Mexican-American identity. *International Review of Modern Sociology, 3*, 192 - 203.

Thorndike, R. M., Cunningham, G. K., Thorndike, R. L., & Hagen, E. P. (1991). *Measurement and evaluation in psychology and education*. New York: Macmillan Publishing Company.

Ting-Toomey, S. (1981). Ethnic identity and close friendship in Chinese-American college students. *International Journal of Intercultural Relations, 5*, 383 - 406.

Torres, I. M., & Gelb, B. D. (2002). Hispanic-targeted advertising: More sales? *Journal of Advertising Research, 42*(6), 69.

Touchstone, E. E., Homer, P. M., & Koslow, S. (1999). Spanish language billboard advertising in the US: Are there effects on Anglos? In F. Bargiela-Chiappini & C. Nickerson (Eds.), *Writing Business Genres, Media and Discourses* (pp. 257 - 272). Essex, UK: Pearson Education Limited.

Triandis, H. C. (1994). *Culture and Social Behavior*. New York: McGraw-Hill.

Triandis, H. C. (1995). *Individualism and collectivism*. Boulder, CO: Westview Press.

Triandis, H. C., Kashima, Y., Hui, H., Lysansky, J., & Marin, G. (1982). Acculturation and biculturalism indices among relatively acculturated Hispanic young adults. *Internamerican Journal of Psychology, 16*, 140 - 149.

Triandis, H. C., Kashima, Y., Shimda, E., & Villareal, M. (1986). Acculturation indices as a means of confirming cultural differences. *International Journal of Psychology, 21*(1), 43 - 70.

Triandis, H. C., McCusker, C., & Hui, C. H. (1990). Multi-method proves of individualism - collectivism. *Journal of Personality and Social Psychology, 59*, 1006 - 1020.

Ueltschy, L. C., & Ryans Jr., J. K. (1997). Employing Standardized Promotion Strategies In Mexico: The Impact Of Language And Cultural Differences. *The International Executive, 39*(4), 479 - 495.

Underhill, P. (1994). Kids in store. *American Demographics, 16*, 22 - 26.

UNRISD. (1999). *Search for Identity: Ethnicity and Political Violence*. Retrieved 12 April, 1999, from http://www.unrisd.org/engindex/publ/list/op/op6/op602.htm

Valencia, H. (1985). Developing an index to measure hispanicness. In E. C. Hirschman & M. B. Holbrook (Eds.), *Advances in Consumer Research* (Vol. 12, pp. 118 - 121). Provo, UT: ACR.

Vallee, F. G. (1982). Inequalities and identity in multi-ethnic societies. In D. Forcese & S. Richer (Eds.), *Social Issues*. Toronto: Prentice Hall.

Verkuyten, M., Hagendoorn, L., & Masson, K. (1996). The ethnic hierarchy among majority and minority youth in the Netherlands. *Journal of Applied Social Psychology, 26*, 1104.

Verkuyten, M., & Kinket, B. (2000). Social distances in a multi ethnic society: The ethnic hierarchy among Dutch preadolescents. *Social Psychology Quarterly, 63*(1), 78 - 85.

Von der Fehr, N. M., & Stevik, K. (1998). Persuasive Advertising and Product Differentiation. *Southern Economic Journal, 65*(1), 113 - 126.

Vos, J. F. J. (2003). Corporate social responsibility and the identification of stakeholders. *Corporate Social - Responsibility and Environmental Management, 10*(3), 141.

Walbott, H. (1995). Congruence, Contagion, and Motor Mimicry: Mutualities in Nonverbal Exchange. In I. Markova & C. Graumann (Eds.), *Mutualities in Dialogue* (pp. 83 - 94). New York: Cambridge University Press.

Walker, D., & Dubitsky, T. M. (1994). Why liking matters. *Journal of Advertising Research, 34*(3), 9 -.

Wallace, J. S. (2003). Value maximization and stakeholder theory: Compatible or not? *The Bank of America Journal of Applied Corporate Finance, 15*(3), 120.

Wallendorf, M., & Reilly, M. (1983). Ethnic migration, assimilation, and consumption. *Journal of Consumer Research, 10*(December), 293 - 302.

Walsh, A. (1990). Becoming an American and liking it as functions of social distance and severity of initiation. *Sociological Inquiry, 60*(2), 177.

Walters, P. G. P. (1986). International marketing policy: A discussion of the standardization construct and its relevance for corporate policy. *Journal of International Business Strategies, 17*(Summer), 55 - 69.

Wassmann, J., & Dasen, P. R. (1998). Balinese spatial orientation: Some empirical evidence of moderate linguistic relativity. *Journal of the Royal Anthropological Institute, 4*(4), 689 - 712.

Watson, J. (1980a). Cultural pluralism, nation-building and educational policies in Peninsular Malaysia. *Journal of Multilingual and Multicultural Development, 1*, 155 - 174.

Watson, J. (1980b). Education and pluralism in South-East Asia, with special reference to Peninsular Malaysia. *Comparative Education, 16*, 139 - 158.

Weber, M. (1961). Ethnic Groups (K. Ferdinand, Trans.). In P. Talcott (Ed.), *Theory of Society* (pp. 301 - 309). New York: Free Press.

Webster, C. (1994). Effects of Hispanic ethnic identification on marital roles in the purchase decision. *Journal of Consumer Research, 21*(2), 319 - 331.

Weiner, N. L. (1974). The effect of education on police attitudes. *Journal of Criminal Justice, 2*, 317 - 328.

Weinfurt, K. P., & Moghaddam, F. M. (2001). Culture and social distance: A case study of methodological cautions. *The Journal of Social Psychology, 141*(1), 101 - 111.

Weinstock, A. A. (1964). Some factors that retard or accelerate the rate of acculturation with special reference to Hungarian immigrants. *Human Relations, 17*(4), 321 - 340.

Wells, W., Burnett, J., & Moriarty, S. (2002). *Advertising* (5 ed.): Prentice Hall.

White, C., & Burke, P. (1987). Ethnic role identity among white and black college students: An interactionist approach. *Sociological Perspectives, 30*, 310 - 331.

Whorf, B. L. (1941). The Relation of Habitual Thought and Behavior to Language. In L. Spier (Ed.), *Language, Culture, and Personality; Essays in Memory of Edward Sapir* (pp. 75 - 93). Menash, WI: Sapir Memorial Publications Fund.

Whorf, B. L. (1956). *Language, Thought and Reality: Selected writings of Benjamin Lee Whorf*. New York: Wiley.

Wierzbicka, A. (1985a). Different cultures, different languages, different speech acts. Polish vs. English. *Journal of Pragmatics, 9*, 145 - 178.

Wierzbicka, A. (1985b). The double life of a bilingual. In R. Sussex & J. Zubrzycki (Eds.), *Polish people and culture in Australia* (Vol. 187 - 223). Canberra: Australian National University.

Wilson, T. C. (1996). Cohort and prejudice: whites' attitudes toward blacks, Hispanics, Jews, and Asians. *The Public Opinion Quarterly, 60*, 253 - 274.

Wind, Y. (1978). Issues and advances in segmentation research. *Journal of Marketing Research, 15*(3), 317 - 337.

Windahl, S., Signitzer, B., & Olson, J. T. (1992). *Using Communication Theory: An introduction to planned communication*. London: Sage Publications.

Worthen, J. B., McGlynn, R. P., Solis, L. Y., & Coats, S. (2002). Proximity attitudes toward objects and people: Reference to a category and a self-representation? *The American Journal of Psychology, 115*(2), 233 - 250.

Wright, M. (1996). The dubious assumptions of segmentation and targeting. *Management Decision, 34*(1), 18 - 24.

Wright, M. J., & Esslemont, D. H. B. (1994). The logical limitations of target marketing. *Marketing Bulletin, 5*, 13 - 20.

Yinger, M. J. (1985). Ethnicity. *Annual Review of Sociology, 11*, 151 - 180.

Zbar, J. D. (1999, Aug 30). Marketing to Hispanics. *Advertising Age, 70,* S1, S20.

Zuengler, J. (1991). Accommodation in Native-nonnative Interactions: Going Beyond the 'What' to the 'Why' in Second Language Research. In H. Giles (Ed.), *Contexts of Accommodation: Developments in Applied Sociolinguistics* (pp. 223 - 244). Cambridge: Cambridge University Press.

Appendix 1: Qualitative Statement for Ads Used In the thesis

Table 1: Comments for Ad Background: Iban. Ad Language: Iban

Ad	Like
1	Like the language that was used in the ad (E58, F, 20,S, I, 4)*. Interesting ethnic background (E259, M, 39,Di, I, 4). Like because use Iban language (E256, M, 35, De, I, 4). First time I read an ad using Iban language (E255, M, 32, De, I, 5). Like because the ad uses Iban language (E252, F, 36, S, I, 5). Cheap price (E251, M, 39, De, I, 4). Use Iban language (E896, F, 20, S, I, 3).
	Dislike
	Don't like because use Iban language and uses a traditional and conservative layout (E15, M, 22, S, M, 6, 4)*. Don't like because don't understand the message (E18, F, 22, Di, C, 5, 2). Don't like because written in Iban, there will be those that won't understand it (E32, F, 22, Di, M, 6, 2). Don't like because don't understand the language at all (E34, F, 20, S, C, 6, 4). the language used is difficult to understand. I don't like language that I don't understand (E86, F, 20, S, M, 5, 2). Don't like the mixture of language like using 'sensasi', try to use more suitable Iban word (E259, M, 39, Di, I, 4). Don't like because this ad too weighted towards the capture of Iban customers hearts (E255, M, 32, D, I, 5). Don't like because leaning too much to one type only, that is focusing on Ibans only. Bahasa Melayu should be used to make it easier for customers of all types of races (E254, F, 34, S, I, 4). too aimed to Iban only and not including other races (E252, F, 36, S, I, 5). No such word as 'sensasi' in Iban (E251, M, 39, D, I, 4). If possible, use Bahasa Malaysia and label as made in Sarawak (E301, M, 37, S, M, 3, 2). Use Bahasa Malaysia (E302, F, 33, S, M, 3, 2). Did not use the official language and difficult to be understood because it is in Iban (E457, F, 24, S, M, 6, 5).

Table 1: Comments for Ad Background: Iban. Ad Language: Iban - continued

Ad	Dislike
1	Not attractive and did not use the official language (E458, M, 43, S, M, 5, 5). Other people will not understand the ads meaning (E459, F, 23, S, I, 4). the language used in the ad is aimed to a certain ethnic group that the company thinks is easier to deceive (E461, M, 40, S, I, 6). the language used is as if it's only for Ibans (E698, F, 20, Di, M, 5, 2). Don't like because the drink in the as is unknown, what type is it, and the Iban language is extremely difficult to understand (E701, F, 49, N, M, 7, 2). the brand is aimed at a specific ethnic group, as a Muslim, I am cautious of its contents (E715, F, 42, S, M, 3, 1). Ad like this shows that this product is specifically for Ibans and that the probability that this drink is alcoholic is high (E896, F, 20, S, I, 3). Not innovative. Only one full advertisement to the Ibans. What kind of advertisement is this? So selfish! Ask yourself is it beneficial to other races. Your success is not on one race business only (E1023, M, 40, De, C, 4, 1). Don't like because this ad is racist. Looks like it emphasizes only Ibans, even though the background is more Malay. I am not confident of this ad (D016, F, 20, S, M, 6, 4). the Iban language is not understood (D030, F, 21, S, C, 6, 2).

* Note: Details beside comments, i.e. (E15, M, 22, S, M, 6, 4) is arranged as follows: Identity No., Sex (M, F), Age, Education (N – No formal education, S- Secondary School, Di – Diploma, De – Degree, M – Masters, P - PhD), Ethnicity (I – Iban, M - Malay, C – Chinese), Ethnic Identity Strength (1 to 7, where 7 is the strongest), Social Distance (1 – 7, where 7 is the furthest social distance).

Table 2: Comments for Ad Background: Iban. Ad Language: Malay

Ad	Like
2	Like because uses Bahasa Melayu and Iban background (E38, F, 22, S, M, 7, 4)*.
	Like because the style of the ad that combines cultural values (E51, M, 20, S, M, 5, 1).
	Like because uses mother tongue (E53, F, 21, S, M, 5, 1).
	Like because there are elements of different races in the ad (E55, F, 21, S, I, 4).
	Like because uses Bahasa Melayu (E65, F, 21, S, M, 5, 1).
	Beautiful, attract attention, language easy to understand, and price shown clearly (E91, F, 20, S, M, 6, 1).
	Very attractive picture of 'pua kumbu' (E143, M, 36, S, C, 4, 1).
	Like because uses 'pua kumbu' background that describes my ethnic group, shows that it's made in Sarawak with a reasonable price (E222, M, 26, D, I, 5).
	I like this ad because this ad is not forcing and has give and take elements between all ethnicities (E321, M, 29, S, M, 5, 1).
	Like because tries to show the image of Ibans through the 'pua kumbu' (E472, M, 24, D, I, 3).
	Like because it's in Bahasa Melayu (D004, F, 20, S, M, 5, 5).

Dislike
Don't like because too simple and uses only Iban ethnic elements. It should use all elements of all ethnicities to make it more pleasing (E25, F, 22, Di, M, 5, 1).
Don't like because it is not in Chinese, so Chinese people cannot understand it (E28, F, 22, S, C, 6, 5).
Don't like because only uses one language, that is Bahasa Melayu. Problems arise when other ethnicities don't understand (E55, F, 21, S, I, 4).
Don't have 'halal' sign (E72, M, 23, Di, M, 6, 1).
No 'halal' logo for Muslims (E91, F, 20, S, M, 6, 2).
Don't like because this ad is not interesting (E99, F, 19, S, M, 5, 4)
This ad is only aimed at one group (E472, M, 24, D, I, 3).
This ad differentiates ethnic groups (E482, F, 36, S, I, 5).
for me, there is nothing here that I like (E628, F, 40, S, M, 4, 4).
Looks like its only suitable for non-Chinese (E847, M, 21, S, C, 7, 2).
This ad is boring. Don't know what it's trying to say. Never tried this tin drink before (D071, M, 21, S, I, 4).

* Note: Details beside comments, i.e. (E15, M, 22, S, M, 6, 4) is arranged as follows: Identity No., Sex (M, F), Age, Education (N – No formal education, S- Secondary School, Di – Diploma, De – Degree, M – Masters, P - PhD), Ethnicity (I – Iban, M - Malay, C – Chinese), Ethnic Identity Strength (1 to 7, where 7 is the strongest), Social Distance (1 – 7, where 7 is the furthest social distance).

Table 3: Comments for Ad Background: Iban. Ad Language: Chinese

Ad	Like
3	Chinese is easier for me to understand (E111, F, 23, S, C, 5, 1)*.
	At least there are some Iban traditional motives (E142, F, 30, Di, I, 3).
	Like the ethnic combination in the graphic image of the ad (E238, F, 25, S, I, 6).
	Multi-ethnic advertising as if one product for all races in Sarawak (E249, M, 37, Di, I, 6).
	the use of 'pua kumbu' that promotes Iban traditions (E248, M, 33, P, I, 4).
	Like because depicts Sarawak identity by the use of the 'pua kumbu.' (E268, F, 45, S, M, 7, 5).
	Dislike
	I am not sure whether it is 'halal' or not (E16, F, 21, S, M, 6, 2).
	Don't like because background of the ad is not suitable and don't attract the attention of the consumer (E24, M, 20, S, C, 7, 5).
	Don't like because don't understand the language (E87, M, 20, S, M, 6, 1).
	Don't like because Chinese language is used (E97, F, 20, S, I, 5).
	Don't like because less honest (E109, F, 22, S, C, 6, 2).
	Less suitable for the Malaysian society because only written in Chinese (E111, F, 23, S, C, 5, 1).
	This ad places too much priority on the Chinese people. I don't understand at all the language used in the ad (E141, M, 20, S, I, 5).
	This ad tried to make the Chinese and Iban as their marketing target. Indirectly, the Ibans are exploited in this ad (E142, F, 30, Di, I, 3).
	What is the content of the tin? Suspicious of its health effects. Not written in Bahasa Melayu. Don't understand when it is nearly 70% written in Chinese (E144, M, 37, S, M, 7, 2).
	Don't like because I don't understand and furthermore it doesn't give correct details (E148, F, 48, S, M, 4, 1).
	Don't like because this ad stands out with one language only. Not everyone understands Chinese (E149, M, 28, S, M, 6, 5).
	Don't like because it's in Chinese (E167, M, 35, D, I, 7).
	the use of language that is not understood by some people may make the message less effective (E238, F, 25, S, I, 6).

Table 3: Comments for Ad Background: Iban. Ad Language: Chinese - continued

Ad	Dislike
3	Don't like because I totally don't understand what is said in the ad. This ad focuses too much on the Chinese as the buyers of the product. Seeing this ad is as if I cannot read. Don't know the real meaning (E239, F, 24, S, I, 6).
	Don't like the use of Chinese because don't understand it (E248, M, 33, P, I, 4).
	This ad is only for one ethnic group (E247, M, 45, S, M, 7, 5).
	This ad places more importance on the understanding and needs of only one ethnic group (E245, F, 33, S, I, 3).
	Don't like because there is only Chinese. Should have romanized language also so that others can understand what is advertised (E268, F, 45, S, M, 7, 5).
	Don't like because don't understand the ad because it is in Chinese (E272, M, 33, Di, M, 7, 1).
	Don't understand Chinese, the type of drink, flavor, what is so great of the drink (E327, M, 35, S, I, 4).
	This ad only uses one language. Only people who understand Chinese will understand what is written (E330, F, 40, S, C, 5, 2).
	Don't like because I don't understand what the ad is saying (E338, F, 49, S, M, 6, 1).
	Don't like because I don't know what this ad is about because the use of language that the ad uses and the drink is liquor and I don't like it (E425, M, 25, S, M, 6, 2).
	Don't understand the ad because it is in Chinese (E452, F, 23, S, M, 5, 2).
	the company that made this ad has little understanding of the multi ethnic society in Malaysia or the drink may be specialized only for the Chinese and is shown in Mandarin newspapers only (E465, F, 44, M, I, 5).
	I feel cautious and not confident towards this ad because it is too simple and the information is aimed only at one race (E496, F, 36, S, I, 7).
	Just use one language that is Chinese. Doesn't depict Malaysia as a multi-ethnic nation (E497, M, 36, Di, I, 5).
	This ad focuses only on the Chinese. too racist. This ad leaves out the Iban as compared to the Chinese (E511, M, 21, S, I, 5).
	This as is aimed only at the Iban and Chinese consumers, whereas in this country, Malays consist of a large portion of consumers (E592, M, 37, S, M, 7, 1).

**Table 3: Comments for Ad Background: Iban. Ad Language: Chinese -
continued**

Ad	Dislike
3	Did not use at all Bahasa Melayu in the ad when Bahasa Melayu is the National Language! (E593, F, 34, Di, M, 7, 1). Other races except Chinese do not understand the ad. Use the National Language! (E599, F, 31, Di, M, 6, 2). Ad uses only Chinese and Chinese is not the national language (E610, F, 35, Di, M, 7, 5). Don't give full information about the product (Halal or not). Can create sensitive racial issues. This is Malaysia not China (D065, F, 25, S, M, 6, 2). Don't like because ad uses Chinese language only (D075, M, 20, S, M, 3, 1). Don't like because ad uses Chinese language only (D077, M, 20, S, M, 3, 1).

* Note: Details beside comments, i.e. (E15, M, 22, S, M, 6, 4) is arranged as follows: Identity No., Sex (M, F), Age, Education (N – No formal education, S- Secondary School, Di – Diploma, De – Degree, M – Masters, P - PhD), Ethnicity (I – Iban, M - Malay, C – Chinese), Ethnic Identity Strength (1 to 7, where 7 is the strongest), Social Distance (1 – 7, where 7 is the furthest social distance).

Table 4: Comments for Ad Background: Iban. Ad Language: Malay & Iban

Ad	Like
4	Like because the background and product design is 70% convincing (E38, F, 22, S, M, 7, 4)*.
	Like because the ad uses our official language that is Bahasa Melayu. Easy to understand, creative, and attracts me to purchase the product (E39, F, 21, Di, M, 5, 5).
	Like because it has portions that reflect the values of Malaysians (E42, F, 19, S, M, 5, 1).
	the use of Bahasa Melayu makes it easy for all races to understand the as. Besides that, the use of Iban makes the Iban people proud a bit (E104, M, 22, S, I5).
	Unique (E264, F, 35, Di, I, 5).
	the advertiser uses Bahasa Melayu as the official language so that all races can understand (E441, F, 26, S, M, 6, 1).

	Dislike
	Don't like because it uses both Iban and Bahasa Melayu (E14, F, 22, Di, C, 6, 6).
	Don't like because did not use Bahasa Melayu completely. Will create suspicion in Malays as to its 'halal'ness and apprehensiveness as to its contents (E29, F, 20, S, M, 7, 5).
	Don't like because not sure if its halal or not because there is no halal sign (E33, F, 22, S, M, 6, 2).
	Don't like because don't have halal sign and it is in dual language (E42, F, 19, S, M, 5, 1).
	Don't like because don't have Chinese language (E43, F, 24, Di, C, 5, 5).
	Don't like because there is no Chinese characters so that Chinese people can understand it (E44, F, 21, S, C, 6, 2).
	Don't like because it may hurt the feelings of other races that don't understand the information in the ad (E62, F, 21, S, C, 5, 2).
	Should place a halal sign so that Malays wont be worried to buy and taste the drink (E63, F, 20, S, M, 7, 4).
	Wary of the product (halal or not) (E66, F, 20, S, M, 7, 2).
	the mixture of language gives the consumer a headache (E111, F, 23, S, C, 5, 1).
	Consumers aren't sure if the product is halal or not, for Muslim (E117, F, 20, S, M, 4, 2).
	Don't like because concentrate on one ethnic group only (Iban) (E161, M, 53, Di, M, 4, 1).
	Not attractive and don't have complete information (E262, F, 24, D, I, 4).

**Table 4: Comments for Ad Background: Iban. Ad Language: Malay & Iban -
continued**

Ad	Dislike
4	Don't like because it is connected to Iban where Iban clothes and 'pua kumbu' is shown together with the drink (E257, F, 35, Di, I, 2).
	Targeted for Ibans only (E429, F, 28, D, M, 6, 2).
	Should have used Bahasa Malaysia only so that other races wont feel left out (E436, F, 24, S, M, 7, 2).
	Don't like incorporating Iban language into the ad (E437, F, 27, S, M, 4, 2).
	the advertiser seems to place an importance on Ibans and maybe this ad is targeted to them (E441, F, 26, S, M, 6, 1).
	This ad can be implicated in political and racial issues; it can also create misunderstanding between the races (E504, M, 36, D, I, 6).
	too many languages used. Just use Bahasa Malaysia. (E579, f, 40, S, M, 6, 1).
	Not quite relevant to Chinese community (E995, F, 40, S, C, 4, 2).
	Don't like because the usage of Bahasa Melayu and Iban is not correct. This shows that the advertiser just wants to sell his product without respecting his customers. This product is aimed at Ibans. (D006, F, 33, Di, I, 5)
	Don't like because not complete that is it does not state whether halal or not for Malays (D026, F, 23, Di, M, 5, 2).
	Don't like because the ad uses multiple languages, should use only Bahasa Melayu (D066, M, 21, S, I, 4).

* Note: Details beside comments, i.e. (E15, M, 22, S, M, 6, 4) is arranged as follows: Identity No., Sex (M, F), Age, Education (N – No formal education, S- Secondary School, Di – Diploma, De – Degree, M – Masters, P - PhD), Ethnicity (I – Iban, M - Malay, C – Chinese), Ethnic Identity Strength (1 to 7, where 7 is the strongest), Social Distance (1 – 7, where 7 is the furthest social distance).

Table 5: Comments for Ad Background: Iban. Ad Language: Malay & Chinese

Ad	Like
5	Like because easier to understand and does not neglect other races (E52, F, 20, S, I, 5)*.
	Like because interesting picture and identifies that the company is owned by Iban (E224, F, 34, D, I, 3).
	Like because the ad shows that we can mix and be friends with others. Shows that Malay, Chinese, and Iban can work together towards unity and cooperation (E357, f, 42, S, M, 4, 2).
	It states the price and is in more than one language (E792, M, 49, D, C, 4, 5).
	Like it because it attempts to involve at least one element (i.e. language) of every ethnic group (E911, F, 23, D, C, 5, 2).
	Like because it mixes 3 races in one ad and easy to understand (D073, M, 23, Di, M, 5, 1).

	Dislike
	Don't like because of the color. Not interesting (E100, M, 21, S, C, 5,2).
	Don't like because the ad is confuses me and I feel cautious to buy this product as the as is from all types of languages (E126, F, 20, S, M, 4, 2).
	Aimed at one ethnic group. Not logical and emphasize too much on one thing. Not fair (E244, F, 26, S, I, 3).
	This ad is not logical (E293, F, 22, S, I, 7).
	Don't place importance on ethnic or culture of a certain society when making a new brand (E303, M, 34, S, I, 5).
	Don't like the use of Chinese (E310, M, 25, S, I, 4).
	the use of Chinese language in the ad is as if there is Chinese traditional substances in the product that makes us unsure of its 'halal'ness for Muslim (E438, F, 26, S, M, 6, 1).
	Aims at a particular group and does not give full information (E443, F, 29, S, M, 5,4).
	It's dull and not eye-catching (E792, M, 49, Di, C, 4, 5).
	the Kain Pua behind doesn't make sense (E911, F, 23, D, C, 5, 2).
	No English statement about the drink (E1026, M, 43, S, C, 4, 1).
	Don't like because does not use an international *lingua franca*, i.e. English. Easier and able to be understood by all (D009, F, 20, S, M, 6, 2).
	Don't have a sign that allows Malays to enjoy it (D073, M, 23, Di, M, 5, 1).

* Note: Details beside comments, i.e. (E15, M, 22, S, M, 6, 4) is arranged as follows: Identity No., Sex (M, F), Age, Education (N – No formal education, S- Secondary School, Di – Diploma, De – Degree, M – Masters, P - PhD), Ethnicity (I – Iban, M - Malay, C – Chinese), Ethnic Identity Strength (1 to 7, where 7 is the strongest), Social Distance (1 – 7, where 7 is the furthest social distance).

Appendix 2: Guinness Malta Point of Sale Promotional Tool

APR 0 1 2009

Printed in the United States
130456LV00006B/129/P

9 783639 061000